and the
POLITICIANS
D1461820

L.B. HACKNEY LIBRARIES
3 8040 005506375

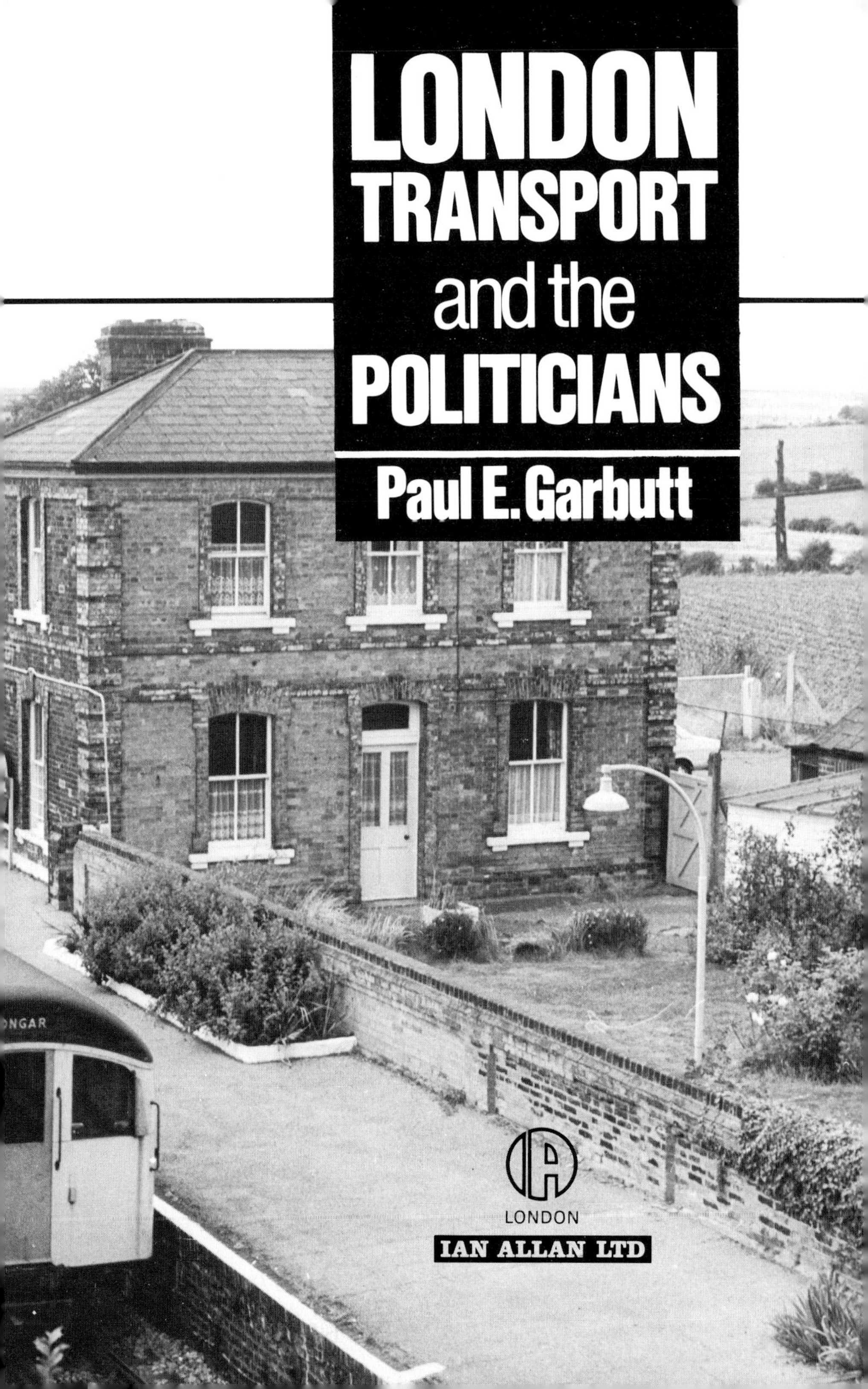

LONDON TRANSPORT and the POLITICIANS

Paul E. Garbutt

IA
LONDON
IAN ALLAN LTD

First published 1985

ISBN 0 7110 1478 7

Published by Ian Allan Ltd, Shepperton, Surrey; and printed by Ian Allan Printing Ltd at their works at Coombelands in Runnymede, England.

Front cover, top:
London Transport's bus-buying policies in the early 1980s were the subject of much controversy. A Leyland Titan crossing Tower Bridge. *Gavin Booth*

Front cover, bottom:
Ken Livingstone seen speaking at a rally in June 1984. *Nigel Farrow*

Back cover, top:
The London Regional Transport HQ at 55 Broadway, London. *London Regional Transport*

Back cover, bottom:
An Epping-Ongar train seen at Ongar in May 1981. *Brian Morrison*

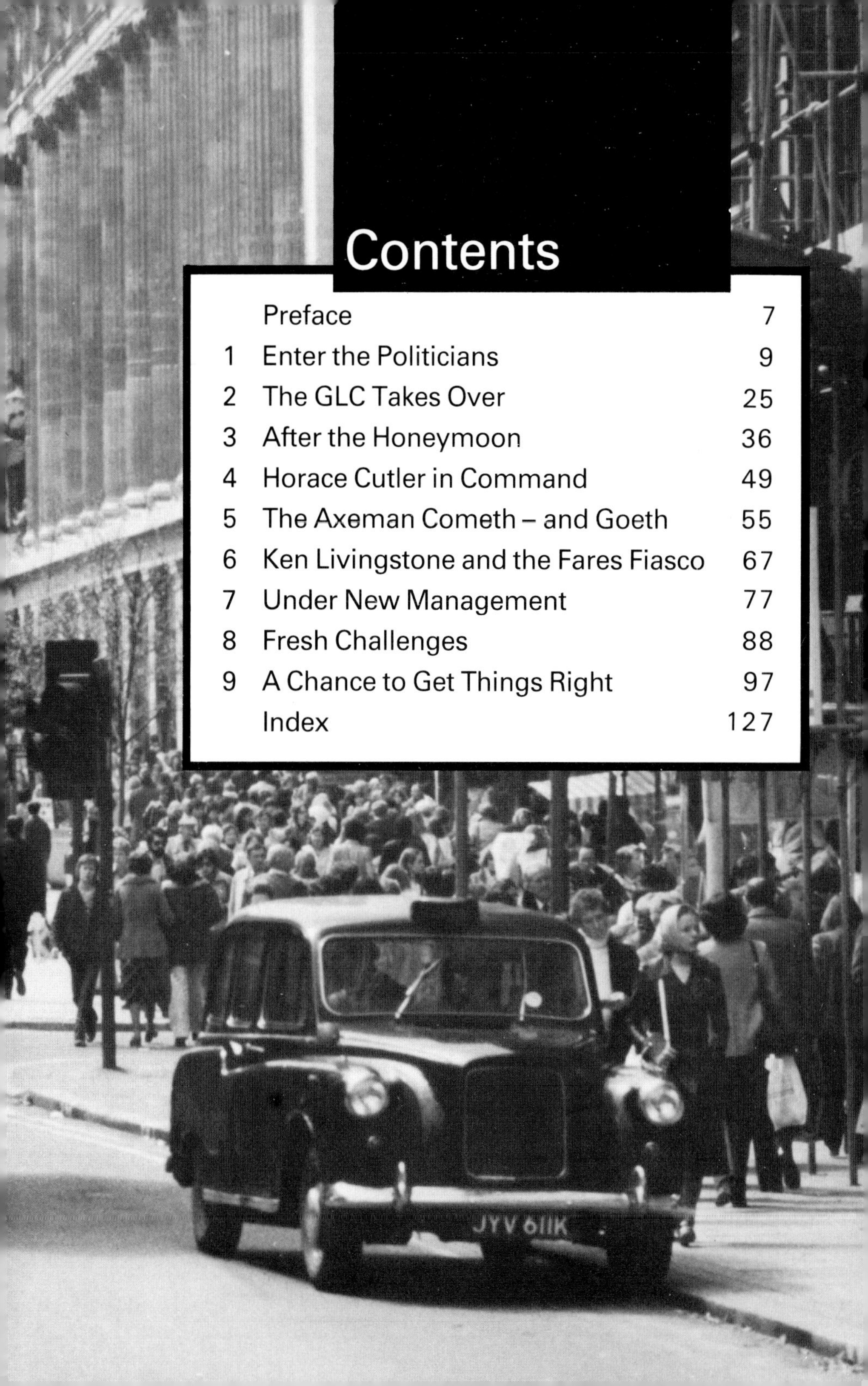

Contents

Preface

This book has been written to show the effects of increased political interference in the affairs of London Transport in the past 20 years or so, particularly while the undertaking was under the policy control of the Greater London Council. A public transport system needs a measure of political control to ensure that its business is conducted on the broad lines of policy for which the electorate has voted. But it does not need political involvement in its professional management to the degree that we have witnessed in London in recent years, nor should it be subjected to radical changes of direction immediately the complexion of its political masters alters.

Without its public transport system, London would quickly grind to a catastrophic halt and millions would be deprived of their sole means of travel. Thus public transport warrants a high and sustained level of financial support. But there must be safeguards to ensure that the public is getting the best value for its money. If there could be a consensus between the main political parties on these basic propositions, London Transport would be better able to get on with its job in the public interest, without much of the sniping and harassment which it has had to suffer in recent years.

I am grateful to a number of people – including several ex-colleagues in London Transport – for their assistance and advice in the preparation of this book. In particular I would like to thank Mr Eric Ellen, Mr Graeme Bruce and Miss Norah King for reading and commenting on the book in draft. I would, however, stress that the views and opinions expressed in the book are my own sole responsibility.

I would like to thank Sir Horace Cutler and his publishers, Messrs Weidenfeld and Nicolson, for permission to quote from his book *The Cutler Files*. Likewise, I am indebted to Mr Leslie Chapman and his publishers, Messrs Chatto and Windus, for permission to quote from his book *Waste Away*.

In respect of the illustrations, I would like to make the following grateful acknowledgements: London Transport (now London Regional Transport); *LT News* (now *LRT News*); Ian Allan Photographic Library; Capital Transport Publishing; BBC Hulton Picture Library; Press Association Photos; London News Agency; British Rail; and Express Newspapers, as credited.

If I have inadvertantly omitted any organisation or person from the list of acknowledgements above, I offer my sincere apologies.

Paul E. Garbutt

Above:
Barbara Castle takes over as Minister of Transport at the end of 1965. *London News Agency*

1 Enter the Politicians

1965 was a critical year for London Transport. In that year, after a long struggle to pay its way, the undertaking bowed to political pressure and for the first time accepted money from the Government as compensation for putting off a fares increase. Thereafter it was to go irretrievably into the red and – because 'he who pays the piper calls the tune' – was to fall more and more under the dubious influence of its paymasters, the politicians.

In 1964 the Greater London Council had come into being as the so-called 'strategic authority' for the whole area of London within the Green Belt. To begin with, the GLC had no responsibility for London Transport; but in 1967 Harold Wilson's Minister of Transport, the tough and pugnacious Barbara Castle, reached an agreement with the Leader of the Conservative GLC, the genial Desmond Plummer, to shift the political and financial control of London Transport from the Government to the Council. This shift duly took place at the beginning of 1970 and was to turn LT into a battleground for the rival local politicians of County Hall.

How was it that a successful enterprise like London Transport, which had broadly paid its way for decades and built up a high reputation for public service not only among Londoners but around the world, could fall on hard times in the 1960s, the era of the 'affluent society'?

Oddly enough, it was the increase in living standards in the 1950s and 1960s which itself led to the decline of London Transport's fortunes. The first few years after the war, when petrol was still rationed and cars were hard to come by, had been peak years for LT. In 1948 the undertaking carried 4,675 million passengers – more than in any year before or since. Moreover many of those passengers were using the buses, trams and Underground trains for trips to the cinema, to sporting events and for shopping – trips made outside the rush hours when the extra services needed to handle them could be provided at little extra cost, using resources of vehicles and staff needed for the peaks which would otherwise have lain idle in the slack hours. In the 1950s this pattern began to change. Petrol was derationed, new cars came off the assembly lines in increasing numbers, and television began to take the place of the cinema and theatre as the main source of public entertainment. As a result, more and more people either used their newly-bought cars for pleasure and shopping journeys, or stayed at home and watched TV.

At the same time, with an increase in the number of people coming into Central London to work each day, and with the introduction of the five-day working week – which led to standard working hours from Mondays to Fridays – the traffic peaks became more and more concentrated.

So London Transport was faced with a worsening situation on two fronts. On the one hand it was losing its profitable off-peak traffic. On the other, it was having to cope with the intensification of its unprofitable peak traffic.

And that was not all. Many new car owners were driving in to work in the central area, causing severe traffic congestion in city streets and jamming narrow thoroughfares with parked vehicles. Bus services were hit severely by the traffic jams. Some buses were so delayed that they had to be turned back before reaching their destination. By 1965 nearly four million bus-miles a year were being 'lost' in this way. The waste of valuable road space by the use of cars for central area commuting was – and remains to this day – appalling. Most cars coming into town carry only one person – the driver – so that 50-60sq ft of precious in-town road space is tied up throughout the working day merely to get one man to his office and back.

Yet another problem facing London Transport in the prosperous 1960s was a shortage of operating staff. Strange though it may sound in to-day's world of recession and mass unemployment, LT was in the 1960s scraping the barrel to find men to keep its services going. By 1965 the undertaking was nearly 2,000 men short of the number needed to drive its red buses, and was losing nearly 20 million bus-miles a year because of the staff shortage.

Despite this there was a serious rise in LT's wage bill, resulting from the heavy wage increases needed to keep the enterprise competitive in the labour market. Another blow was the loss of many valuable passengers who abandoned the buses because of the unreliability of the undermanned services. Some of these passengers took to their own cars, so increasing street congestion and further hampering the operation of the buses. The result was a vicious downward spiral which in the end benefited nobody.

Already, in the early 1960s, London Transport was warning the Government of the day that the successive fare rises needed to keep up with rising costs – especially labour costs – were proving more and more self-defeating, and that the undertaking was finding it increasingly hard to reconcile the two main duties laid on it by Parliament – to provide an adequate service to the travelling public of London, and at the same time to pay its way. Even before 1965, although London Transport's revenue was still covering its working costs and interest charges, the surpluses earned were falling short of the targets set by the Government.

Little credit was given to London Transport for holding out so long before finally going into the red. It was the last of the world's great city transport systems to do so. The Paris and New York undertakings, for example, had been heavily subsidised for years previously, not only in respect of capital but also on revenue account. Some city transport departments abroad enjoyed hidden financial support which it was difficult to identify in their published accounts. Some were cross-subsidised from other municipal enterprises, such as power supply, which were run at a profit.

Until 1962 the links between London Transport and the Government had been fairly tenuous. In the postwar nationalisation of transport, LT became an operating subsidiary of the cumbersome British Transport Commission. Naturally the Commission was preoccupied with the enormous problems of British Railways, which had emerged from the war in an exhausted and run-down state. By comparison the much smaller London Transport system received only limited attention, especially as it was not causing endless financial headaches. In effect there were two barriers between LT and the politicians – the British Transport Commission and the civil servants in the Ministry of Transport. It was not often that London Transport's problems were considered serious enough to be taken right up to the national political level for decision, although LT was subjected to the attentions of an official committee of inquiry (the Chambers Committee) in the mid-1950s. Perhaps the biggest step taken by the Government on a London Transport issue in this period was the authorisation in 1962 of the construction of the Victoria Line, destined to benefit millions of travellers for generations to come.

On 1 January 1963, following the Tory Government's Transport Act of 1962, the

British Transport Commission was abolished and its over-extended empire was broken up. London Transport emerged as a separate Board, legally owning the assets which it operated, and responsible to the Minister of Transport for the broad conduct of its affairs. By cutting out the Commission as an intermediary, this change brought LT one step closer to its political masters. But London Transport was still a 'small fish in a large pool' so far as the Government was concerned, and – at least until the undertaking began to lose money on any scale – most of its management contacts with Whitehall were with senior civil servants rather than with Ministers.

Alec (later Sir Alec) Valentine was the Chairman of London Transport at the time of its 1963 transformation and for a few years thereafter. Originally one of Frank Pick's proteges in the heyday of the old prewar London Passenger Transport Board (LPTB) under the famous Ashfield Pick regime, Valentine had charge of the operating and commercial departments – as well as most of the engineering departments – of LT just after nationalisation. Then he went away to become a Member of the British Transport Commission, returning as Chairman of LT in 1959. Valentine had a fine brain and a great penchant for detail; he was at his best when giving evidence on some complicated issue before a tribunal or inquiry. His qualities were less suited to the role of Chairman, and in his later years in that office he was in any case a sick man. So he tended to withdraw more and more into the 'ivory tower' of the vast Chairman's Room at 55 Broadway, leaving his Vice-Chairman, Arthur Grainger – a fatherly figure with a fund of sound common sense – to preside over the day-to-day affairs of the undertaking.

In 1965 Valentine was succeeded by Maurice (later Sir Maurice) Holmes, previously Chairman of the Tilling bus group, who had been a practising barrister before entering the field of public transport management. A jaunty extrovert, Holmes had a very different style from that of his predecessor; but he never seemed quite at home in the chairmanship of LT and relied much on the support of his Vice-Chairman, Anthony Bull. Bull was a reserved but highly effective administrator who had been – like Valentine – a prewar protege of Frank Pick, and had returned to LT as the personnel manager after outstanding military service on the Army Staff during the war.

Maurice Holmes received a knighthood in the Birthday Honours of 1969, following the opening of the main section of the Victoria Line earlier in that year. But neither the then Labour Minister of Transport, Richard Marsh, nor the Conservative GLC leader, Sir Desmond Plummer, offered any encouragement to Holmes to think that he would stay in the chair at London Transport after the undertaking was transferred to GLC control. So he stepped down at the end of 1969, with compensation for the short uncompleted period of his five-year term of office. Holmes must have been dismayed at his rapid change in fortunes, from being knighted in June to being dropped from his job in December. However, he was subsequently asked to reorganise and streamline the operation of the Courts of Justice in the South Eastern Circuit, and that task must certainly have been more congenial to him than occupying the hot seat at 55 Broadway.

The successive Ministers of Transport who had the ultimate political responsibility for London Transport in the middle and late 1960s were a mixed bag. Up to the fall of the Douglas-Home Government in the autumn of 1964, the flamboyant Ernest Marples was the Minister; he is best remembered by his habit of cycling round central London. With the advent of the first Wilson Government, the Ministry was awarded to the little-known Tom Fraser. However, when Harold Wilson made some Cabinet changes in 1965, he effectively upgraded the Department of Transport by appointing as its head a controversial national figure, Barbara Castle. With

Left:
Sir Alec Valentine, Chairman of LT when it came under Government control in 1963.
London Transport

Below:
Sir Maurice Holmes, Chairman of LT 1965-69.
London Transport

Above:
Tom Fraser, Transport Minister in 1965, starts a prototype automatic train on the Woodford-Hainault line. Maurice Holmes looks on. *London Transport*

Right:
Richard Marsh (now Lord Marsh), Minister of Transport 1968-69. *British Rail*

characteristic energy she set about preparing a compendious programme of change across the whole field of land transport, culminating in one of the longest acts on the Statute book, the Transport Act of 1968. Among its many provisions that Act set up the present public transport undertakings in the big provincial city areas such as Greater Manchester and Merseyside, and gave the Government and local authorities power to make capital grants towards the cost of public transport improvement schemes.

In 1968 Barbara Castle was succeeded as Minister of Transport by Richard (now Lord) Marsh, who was at that time still not widely known. He was to come to the fore when, after being sacked from the Cabinet by Harold Wilson in 1969, he emerged as a contentious and rather trouble-prone Chairman of British Rail in the 1970s. During his short period as Transport Minister he secured the passage of the Transport (London) Act of 1969, which gave effect to the unnatural agreement of two years earlier between Barbara Castle and Desmond Plummer for the transfer of London Transport to GLC control. Marsh's one previous connection with the affairs of London Transport had been less exalted; nearly 20 years earlier, he had spent six months analysing LT staff statistics to find out why bus drivers were particularly prone to broken ankles and piles.

Then, for a brief period between 1969 and the fall of Harold Wilson's Government in May 1970, the Transport portfolio (now downgraded again) was held by Fred Mulley, whose biggest moment of public notice was to come later, when, as Defence Secretary in the Callaghan Government, he was quite literally caught napping while sitting with the Queen on the dais during the Silver Jubilee Review of the RAF.

One feature of the period during which London Transport came under the direct political control of the Minister (1963-69) was the generally good liaison between LT and British Rail on the many questions affecting them jointly in and around London – fares, the co-ordination of services, interchange facilities, new works and so on. Although after the break-up of the British Transport Commission in 1962 the two undertakings no longer formed part of the same organisation, they were still subject to the direction of the same political body – the Government – so that their activities continued to reflect a common political philosophy. One possible source of friction between British Rail and LT had been eliminated on the eve of the BTC break-up; the two undertakings had agreed on how to divide between them the ownership of the lines, stations and other installations in the London area in which they had a joint interest – for example, the Gunnersbury-Richmond line, the Putney Bridge-Wimbledon line and the tracks carrying the District Line trains to Upminster. This division of ownership was, however, not immutable; under the terms of the 1962 Act, the two Boards were able to amend these 'vestings' by agreement later if they so desired, and one such change occurred at the beginning of 1969, when the whole of the local line to Upminster passed into LT's ownership. Close liaison between LT and BR in the 1963-69 period was assured not only by frequent meetings between the two Chairman but also by an effective structure of joint committees for day-to-day problems and long-term planning.

It is perhaps significant that the coming of Harold Wilson's first Government in October 1964 should have been followed in May 1965 by the first direct Government intervention into the financial affairs of London Transport. That intervention took the form of a request – in effect an order – to LT from the Government to defer an increase in fares which had been planned for 2 May. Admittedly LT had been giving warnings that it was finding it increasingly difficult to pay its way, let alone reach the financial targets agreed with the previous administration to meet the terms of the

1962 Act. Admittedly, too, all but £1million of LT's deficit for the year 1965 was cancelled out by a Government payment of nearly £4million as compensation to LT for the fares freeze. Nevertheless, this Government intervention of 1965 can now be seen as the start of a series of politically-inspired ups and downs of London Transport fares, culminating in the ridiculous see-sawing of fare levels which London has witnessed in the last few years.

The deferred fares rise was allowed to take place in January 1966, but it was by then too low to recover the increase in costs which had occurred in the meanwhile. So the Government put through a special Transport Finances Act during 1966 to enable it to make revenue grants to London Transport, and eventually picked up the bill for a deficit of nearly £6million for the year.

There was a further Government-imposed freeze on LT fares in 1967 and it was not until the second half of 1968 that the next round of fares increases was authorised. Thus, as a direct result of Government policy, LT fares had remained unchanged for over 2½ years, during a period when the undertaking's costs – especially wage costs – had risen steadily. As prices generally were increasing during the period (despite the Government's prices and incomes legislation at the time), the fares freeze meant that the passenger was getting, in real terms, a progressively cheaper ride.

All this was in line with the Wilson Government's stated policy towards public transport. In 1965 a Commons Select Committee which had reviewed London Transport's problems urged that public transport should be given greater priority and that LT should be equipped with better tools to do the job. In its White Paper on the Select Committee's findings, the Government set out a number of objectives, including the maintenance and improvement of public transport as an essential service, and the achievement of a 'more equitable distribution of the burden of paying for London's transport in all its forms'. As an expression of those aims, the 1966-68 fares freeze certainly seems to have had a fair measure of success. There had been a fall of 5% or 6% per annum in the number of LT passengers in the years preceding the freeze. In 1967, when fares were frozen throughout the year, the decline in the passenger figure was less than ¼%; and even in 1968, the second half of which saw the end of the freeze, the drop in traffic on LT was only 1.5%.

The Wilson Government was also committed to making grants towards the capital cost of public transport improvement schemes. In a further White Paper on transport policy in 1966, it pointed out that the Government already contributed heavily to the cost of building and improving main roads in towns and cities, and argued that it was only fair that it should have the power to help in the same way to pay for new or improved urban rail and bus facilities.

As mentioned earlier, the legislation to make this possible was included in Barbara Castle's massive Transport Act of 1968. The Government had already announced the types of project that would attract the new capital grants. They included schemes for new or improved city and suburban railways, interchange facilities, station car parks and bus stations. Of course, before getting the grants, the operators had to show that their projects fitted into the planned development for all forms of transport in the areas concerned. Grants were also announced for the purchase of new buses, provided that these were of types approved by the Ministry of Transport. The purpose of these bus grants was to help make the bus more attractive in comparison with the private car, and to raise productivity in the bus industry by helping to get more one-man-operated buses into service as soon as possible; but the proviso about bus types was to have some unfortunate results for London Transport, since many of the approved 'off-the-peg' buses, while adequate for most provincial and rural services, could not stand up to the wear and tear experienced in the exceptionally arduous traffic conditions of London.

London Transport was quick off the mark in applying for the capital infrastructure and bus grants as soon as they became available, and received nearly £13½million from this source in the first two years of the grant scheme (1968 and 1969). British Rail, whose suburban lines also qualified for the infrastructure grants, was slower to react, so that LT tended at first to hog these new capital funds.

The Transport Act of 1968 provided yet another source of financial aid to public transport operators in the form of research and development grants. These were to prove a great help to the operators and the transport supply industry in devising new methods and equipment to improve passenger comfort and convenience, and to cut operating costs. These grants were also to have a spin-off in promoting British exports; more and more cities abroad were having to build costly underground railways to help combat their growing street traffic problems, and multi-million pound export orders were waiting for the countries and manufacturers able to supply the most modern, efficient and reliable equipment for the many new metro networks coming into existence around the world.

From the beginning of 1969, a further Government boost was given to public transport by an additional rebate on the fuel duty paid by regular bus service operators. This cut London Transport's fuel tax bill by over £1million a year.

One sizeable item which LT was having to pay each year out of its operating revenue was the interest on its accumulated capital debt. When LT was put directly under the aegis of the Government in 1963, the undertaking's capital debt was fixed at £162million. This was not large in relation to the size of the undertaking, mainly because most of the Underground tunnels had been built back in Victorian and Edwardian days, when costs were tiny by modern standards. In 1963 the interest that had to be paid on this capital debt was just under £5¾million. By the end of 1969 LT's last year under direct Government control, the capital debt had risen to £270million – thanks largely to the building of the Victoria Line in the intervening years – and the annual interest charge had doubled, to nearly £11½million.

From 1968 onwards much of LT's new capital expenditure was being repaid in the form of infrastructure and bus grants; but that still left the accumulated capital of the past to be serviced. So Plummer and his Conservative GLC made it a condition of their takeover of responsibility for London Transport in 1970 that the whole of LT's capital debt at the time of the takeover should be written off by the Government. With this relief, and with grants from the Government and the GLC to offset much of the new capital expenditure, it was expected that London Transport would from 1970 onwards be able to cover its annual costs from its revenue and even earn a small surplus. LT's annual report for 1967, the year when the Castle-Plummer bargain was struck, sounded a note of pious hope. 'When the financial reconstruction has taken place', it said 'and an appropriate level of fares has been established, there is no reason why the undertaking should not be self-supporting again if the right steps are taken to enable its services to move freely.'

Unfortunately the two main political factions in the Greater London Council differed strongly – as they still do – on fare levels and on priorities for public transport. The Conservatives had already insisted that, as a further condition of their taking responsibility for London Transport in 1970, the fares freeze of 1966-68 must end; the resultant fare increases in August/September 1968 and September/November 1969, were imposed to enable LT to go into its new incarnation with an operating surplus, despite the effect on traffic. Labour councillors were more interested in giving priority to public transport and keeping down fares, despite operating losses and higher rates. In any case, social and economic factors were to go on working against London Transport in the 1970s, and it was not many years after the GLC takeover that all hope of keeping LT in operational surplus had to be abandoned.

In addition to the financial change involved in the GLC takeover of London Transport, a big structural change had to be made. Ever since the original London Passenger Transport Board had been set up in 1933, the undertaking had operated in a special area, known as the London Passenger Transport Area, covering about 2,000sq miles and stretching from Stevenage in the north to Horsham in the south, and from Slough in the west to Gravesend in the east. The outer part of this area was served by London Transport's green 'Country Buses and Coaches', and the inner part – roughly corresponding to the later GLC area – by the Underground and red 'Central Buses'. With the transfer of London Transport to GLC control, LT's operating area was cut down to that of the Council (about 600sq miles), and the whole of the Country Bus & Coach Department was hived off to form a subsidiary of the National Bus Company under the title of London Country Bus Services Limited. London Transport was left with the Underground and the red buses. The traffic lost to LT as a result of this change amounted to just under 10% of the 1969 passenger-mileage.

This reduction in the size of London Transport's operating area may have looked right at the time, but it seems less sensible in retrospect. The Greater London Council's area does not embrace the whole Metropolitan region dependent on London, but is limited to the built-up area within the Green Belt. All through the 1950s and 1960s, with official encouragement, a shift of population was going on from the Greater London area to the outer metropolitan zone beyond the Green Belt. Many of the people in this outer zone travel to Central London and back each day for their work, using British Rail to get to town and London Transport to move about within the central area. So, in terms of the overall pattern of public transport, the old London Passenger Transport Area made much more sense than the GLC area does. Indeed it may be questioned whether the GLC area was from the start not too small for other purposes too. A comparison with Greater Manchester for example, or the Strathclyde Region of Scotland, is revealing. Greater Manchester, with less than 40% of the population of Greater London has over 80% of the area. Strathclyde (centred on Glasgow), with only a third of the population of Greater London, has an area nearly nine times larger.

Also it seems unfair, with many daily users of LT services coming from the outer zone beyond the Greater London boundaries, that any rates burden which may have to be imposed to maintain adequate LT services should be borne wholly by the GLC ratepayers.

There is the further argument that the maintenance of good London Transport services is essential to the success of London as a seat of government, a commercial and financial centre of world importance, and a great tourist attraction. London is unlike all provincial cities in that decisions taken there and trade deals made there can affect the lives of every man, woman and child in the country. So it is not unfair that the general British taxpayer should share with the London ratepayer the bill for any financial support needed to keep the essential services of London, such as its public transport, running effectively and well.

While London Transport and the Greater London Council were getting ready for the takeover of the one by the other, LT's operational difficulties continued to mount. Despite substantial wage rises and recruiting drives (not only in Britain but also in Ireland and the West Indies) the shortage of operating staff by 1969 was

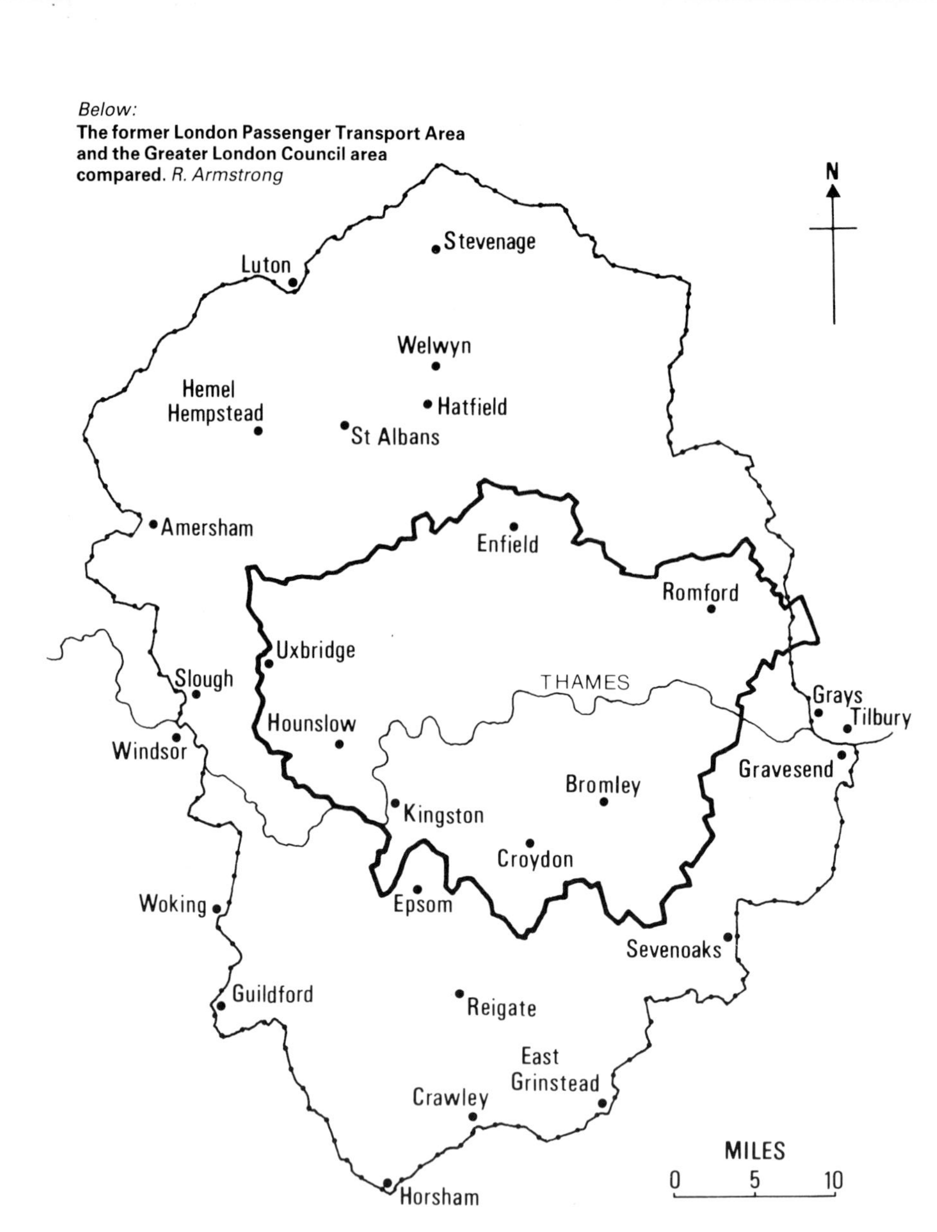

Below:
The former London Passenger Transport Area and the Greater London Council area compared. *R. Armstrong*

severe. By September of that year, the shortage of bus drivers and conductors over the whole red bus fleet was between 18% and 19%, and at the worst garages in the west and northwest of London the figure was over 30%. Inevitably there were serious gaps and irregularities in the bus services, despite overtime working and strenuous day-to-day efforts to keep delays down to a minimum. The Underground was less severely hit, although cuts had to be made in peak-hour services on some lines in the winter of 1968-69 because of staff shortages.

Meanwhile there was little let-up in LT's other great operational problem, traffic congestion. The gradual strangulation of the in-town bus services by private cars in the postwar era is illustrated by comparing the numbers of road vehicles and their occupants entering Central London during the morning peak period in 1952 and in 1969. In those 17 years, the number of cars coming in went up from 30,000 to over 71,000, while the number of buses went down from nearly 7,000 to only 4,000; but because the private car, usually with only one occupant, is so wasteful of road space compared with the bus, the total number of people coming into Central London by road in the peak period actually went down from 314,000 in 1952 to 266,000 in 1969. Moreover it was not only in the central area and its approaches that traffic congestion was strangling bus services and cutting down the flow of people; by the 1960s, suburban centres around London were becoming similarly jammed up.

There was one further headache for London Transport in the run-up to the GLC takeover, namely the planned conversion to decimal currency, for which 15 February 1971 was fixed as 'D-day'. LT, which carries out millions of small transactions every day – many involving change-giving – was naturally greatly affected by the decimal currency proposals, and in the middle 1960s pressed the Government to reconsider its decision to go ahead with the £1/new penny system. LT's objections to this particular system were that it lacked a close relationship with the old currency at the lower denominations, would be difficult to phase in during the run-up to the changeover, was likely to delay transactions, and would cause difficulty in the conversion of ticket machines. London Transport was supported in these protests by other public transport operators, but its objections were overruled by the Wilson Government and the £1/new penny scheme went ahead unchanged.

London Transport did not stand idly by as the problems mounted, but attacked them with a series of positive schemes. In 1964 agreement was reached with the Transport & General Workers' Union on steps to save manpower and vehicles by introducing one-man-operated buses on suburban routes and larger buses on suitable central area routes. Early in 1966, the first Red Arrow one-man-operated single-deck flat-fare buses began running on a short heavily-loaded route between Victoria and Marble Arch. Then, later in the same year, LT announced an ambitious plan to reshape the whole of the London bus system by introducing more Red Arrow routes, curtailing some of the longer trunk routes between the suburbs and the centre to counter the effects of traffic congestion, turning local suburban routes into feeders to the trunk routes, railway stations and suburban centres (using one-man buses, with flat fares), and eventually converting the longer suburban routes to one-man operation as well. When it was first announced, this reshaping plan was hampered by regulations which forbade the use of one-man-operated double-deck buses and resulted in LT orders for single-deck buses in considerable numbers. However, the Ministry withdrew these regulations in 1967, and by 1970 London Transport was proclaiming – wrongly, as it turned out – that its entire bus fleet would be one-man-operated within a decade.

On the Underground, the biggest development of the 1960s was the building of the Victoria Line, which had been advocated strongly by London Transport and was expected, among other things, to help in relieving road traffic congestion by attracting people away from their cars. Also there were innovations on the new line which, if they could be extended to other parts of the Underground, should save manpower and operating costs, and claw back some of London Transport's lost revenue. One was automatic train operation – ATO – which cuts out the need for

Above:
Driver-only cars block crowded buses: a scene from Elephant & Castle in 1966. *London Transport*

Left:
Maurice Holmes (LT Chairman), Stephen Swingler, MP and Barbara Castle inspect a new Red Arrow bus in 1966. *London Transport*

guards and leaves only one man in charge of a train, to act as a lookout, to operate the doors at stations and to set the train in motion; every other function is automatic. The other innovation was automatic fare collection – AFC – designed to reduce the number of ticket collecting staff and cut down on fraudulent travel. Other initiatives on the Underground included increasing and expanding the car parks for park-and-ride passengers at suburban stations (raising the total number of car spaces from 4,000 to 11,000 in six years), and modernising the big power station at Lots Road, Chelsea (cutting the cost of the current generated there by 25% per unit in seven years).

During the 1960s London Transport also kept up pressure on the Ministry of Transport and local authorities to do all that they could, by way of road improvements and so-called traffic engineering schemes, and by more control of parking, to ease street congestion and keep the traffic moving. Between 1958 and 1963 most of the central area had become a controlled parking zone, to the great benefit of the traffic there. But the very success of the parking meters and traffic wardens in Central London led to more congestion in the inner suburbs in the peak hours, causing long delays to buses. So new schemes had to be brought in to unclog the approaches to the central area and give the buses – the most efficient users of road space in terms of passengers carried – some measure of priority. Among these schemes were the new urban clearways, more one-way systems, and – towards the end of the 1960s – the first experimental 'bus only' lanes. Also, parking controls began to be introduced in congested suburban centres. If these steps did not greatly improve the running of the buses, they did at least prevent the services from getting worse as car ownership continued to build up.

Not all the initiatives taken by London Transport in the 1960s were to prove wholly successful in the 1970s. In some cases, such as the bus reshaping plan and the Underground AFC scheme, LT was to find that it had bitten off rather more than it could chew. Nevertheless the results achieved were not negligible. For example, the number of bus-miles run by one-man-operated buses went up from eight million in 1964 to 24 million in 1970; and by 1981 it was to rise to 84 million, or nearly one-half of the total bus-mileage operated. London Transport at least deserves the credit for having responded with some vigour to the mounting challenge of the 1960s.

In the critical years of the mid-1960s the politicians had two opportunities to put London Transport under the microscope. The first came in 1965, when – as mentioned earlier – the Commons Select Committee on Nationalised Industries carried out a full inquiry into LT's problems and activities. In its report the Commons Committee supported what London Transport was doing to improve and extend services and to cut down on manpower, but it criticised the way in which a number of particular issues had been dealt with by LT, by the former British Transport Commission and by previous Ministers of Transport. Its conclusion was that if the conditions under which LT operated were improved by subsidised capital improvements, priorities for buses on the roads, more automated equipment and greater staff productivity, and if the Board showed the 'necessary foresight and drive', then London Transport should in time be able to provide 'an efficient, economic and adequate service of public transport throughout their Area, for which the travelling public would be willing to pay.' The report was by no means a whitewash operation, but it did show some sympathy with LT's position as the victim of economic and social forces largely beyond its own control. To the Committee's particular criticisms, London Transport delivered a spirited reply, which was laid before the House along with the Select Committee's report. In the subsequent Commons debate, the Minister of Transport confirmed that the

Above:
The Victoria Line opening, 1969. With the Queen on the inaugural train are Maurice Holmes, Eric Wilkins and Anthony Bull of LT, and Richard Marsh, Transport Minister. *London Transport*

Below:
Ticket gates in the new station concourse, Oxford Circus, 1969. *London Transport*

Government was committed to improving public transport in London and discouraging the use of private cars in peak hours.

The politicians' second chance to put London Transport through the hoop came when, in the following year, the Government set up a joint enquiry with LT to look into the undertaking's financial, commercial, operating and management problems. Two firms of private consultants were brought in to help in the review, which was master-minded by Stephen Swingler, MP. The report of the team directing the review was not ready until the beginning of 1968, by which time the Castle-Plummer agreement on the transfer of LT to GLC control had already been reached. So the Government decided to publish a White Paper in the summer of 1968, incorporating and commenting on the inquiry report, and setting out its proposals for the Transport (London) Act of 1969. On the results of the inquiry, the White Paper had these comments:

'Judged against transport undertakings in large cities abroad which provide a similarly comprehensive range of services, London Transport have done well. They have so far had no capital grants for investment expenditure. Fares, though often criticised, are lower than in many foreign undertakings. They have gone up less, compared with pre-war, than prices in many industries which do not face the same combination of adverse circumstances: a labour-intensive service industry hit by falling demand and by a rapidly worsening operating environment.'

As the deadline for the transfer of London Transport to the policy control of the Greater London Council approached, there were doubts about the continued co-operation between the four main parties involved in transport in London – the Ministry, the GLC, London Transport and British Rail – under the new order. A pompously-titled 'Transport Co-ordinating Council for London' had been set up in 1966, with representation from the four bodies, as well as the London Boroughs and the TUC; but it had no real authority and proved something of a paper tiger. During 1969, after consulting the main interests involved, the GLC published its Greater London Development Plan; London Transport pressed for a clear statement of priority for public transport in the Plan, in view of the efficient use which buses and trains made of scarce and costly resources compared with their main rival, the private car. Under the 1969 Act the GLC was also given the duty of preparing and publishing regular Transport Plans for Greater London, intended to strike the right balance between the claims of public and private transport. To help the Council to carry out this demanding task, a Greater London Transport Planning Group (comprising GLC, Ministry, LT and BR representatives) was set up well before the deadline for the Council's takeover of LT.

As mentioned earlier, London Transport and British Rail saw eye-to-eye on most matters during the 1960s – partly, at least, because they had the same political master, the Government. However, there was one question on which they did not agree – the question of how Heathrow Airport should be served by rail. London Transport thought that the Piccadilly Line of the Underground should be extended for 3½ miles from Hounslow West to the centre of the Airport, which would thus be 'plugged in' to the whole 240-mile Underground network. British Railways thought that it would be better to serve the airport by a spur from the Southern Region line at Feltham, which would enable a special service of airport trains to be run non-stop between Victoria and Heathrow. In 1966 the Transport Co-ordinating Council for London reviewed the two schemes and recommended (London Transport alone dissenting) that the British Rail scheme should be adopted. The operator of

Heathrow Airport, the British Airports Authority, also favoured the BR scheme, and its chairman, Sir Peter Masefield – who will appear in a different role later in this book – publicly endorsed it. However, the Minister of Transport had not finally made up his mind, and played for time by allowing both LT and BR to apply for the Parliamentary powers needed for their respective schemes in the 1966-67 Parliamentary Session.

The next milestone in the saga of the Heathrow rail link was the appointment of Ralph Bennett to a seat on the board of London Transport. Bennett, a rotund and buoyant character with an optimistic outlook on life, had been managing the Manchester bus system and had a long experience of dealing with local politicians. Bennett's post in London Transport included responsibility for planning, and he was soon pressing for the Heathrow rail link issue to be reopened. In any case, the traffic demands of Heathrow were growing rapidly and the need for a rail link to the airport was becoming more and more urgent. So in the autumn of 1969 the Government set up a special body, the Heathrow Link Steering Group, to study the whole question afresh and come up with the best solution. The Group consisted of representatives of the Ministries, local authorities and main British airlines involved, the British Airports Authority, British Rail and London Transport. The Group was well chaired by a senior civil servant from the Ministry of Transport, John (now Sir John) Garlick, who later became Permanent Secretary in the Cabinet Office. The BR scheme started as favourite, but a full cost-benefit and financial assessment of the two alternatives showed, rather surprisingly, a clear advantage for the Underground scheme. There were several reasons for this. One was that virtually all the passengers using the proposed BR service to Victoria would have to change there to Underground, bus or taxi to reach their final destination, whereas the LT option would link the airport directly into the entire Underground system; moreover, many air passengers' destinations – including the main hotel districts in inner and central London – could be reached direct by the Piccadilly Line from the airport, without changing. A further factor was that the Underground service would be a good deal more frequent than the BR service. Yet another reason was that serious problems emerged when the arrangements for the Victoria check-in associated with the BR option came to be planned in detail. The long and short of it was that the Steering Group finally recommended the Underground extension scheme.

Despite its heavy capital cost, the Heathrow extension was clearly going to be profitable to London Transport from the start, since the passengers using it would travel well beyond the extension itself, and so bring more revenue to the rest of the Underground system. Nevertheless, in approving the scheme, the Greater London Council decided to make a grant of 25% of the capital cost, and the Government later made a further 25% grant on the grounds of the line's national importance. So LT was left to meet only the remaining 50% of the cost itself.

The Heathrow Underground link was to produce an odd quirk of fate. In January 1973 – when he was no longer Chairman of the Airports Authority – Sir Peter Masefield was appointed a part-time board member of London Transport, in which role he had to help in monitoring the progress of the scheme which he had earlier opposed.

2 The GLC Takes Over

The transfer of the policy and financial control of London Transport from the Government to the GLC took place as planned on 1 January 1970. On balance, the auguries for the success of the new set-up looked deceptively good. Granted, London Transport's operational area had been unnaturally curtailed. But the undertaking was now directly linked with the elected body responsible for strategic planning and for the main road system of Greater London. Moreover, the multi-million-pound burden of meeting the annual interest charges on its capital debt had been lifted from LT's back; and much of LT's future capital expenditure was likely to be met by infrastructure and bus grants from the Government and the Council. The new Victoria Line was already open from northeast London through the central area to Victoria, and looked like fulfilling all LT's hopes for it; and the extension from Victoria to Brixton was under construction.

To preside over the fortunes of London Transport in its third incarnation within eight years, the Council appointed as Chairman a distinguished civil servant who had risen through the ranks, without the benefit of Oxbridge, to become Permanent Under-Secretary at the War Office and then Permanent Secretary at the Ministry of Aviation. This was Sir Richard Way, widely known as Sam Way, who bore little resemblance to the traditional Whitehall mandarin and was to prove one of the best chairmen that London Transport had ever had. Alert and decisive, with a puckish sense of humour and a ready twinkle in the eye, he quickly stamped his authority on the LT management and endeared himself to the staff by studying their problems and championing their legitimate interests. Between his civil service career and his chairmanship of LT, Sam Way had led the board of a large firm of forklift truck manufacturers, so that he also had useful commercial experience and knew what was due to the public not only as users of the buses and Underground but also as, in effect, LT's 'shareholders'. Dealing with the GLC politicians – of both main parties – caused Sam Way some annoyance but few qualms; having played in the premier league of Whitehall politics, he found little difficulty in coping with the second-division sides fielded by County Hall.

Although the main political control of London Transport was in the hands of the Greater London Council for nearly 15 years, Central Government retained a considerable measure of influence on LT affairs through the provision of capital and other grants, its legislation programme on urban transport generally, and its control of British Railways. The changing state of relations between Central Government and the GLC has therefore been a matter of no little importance to London Transport.

Since 1970 the Government and the GLC have been of the same political complexion as each other (both Conservative or both Labour) for 50% of the time; for the remaining 50%, administrations of opposing views have glared across the Thames at each other from Whitehall and County Hall. One might expect London Transport to be less of a political battlefield when the Prime Minister and GLC

Above:
Sir Richard Way, Chairman of LT 1970-74.
London Transport

Leader belong to the same party; generally this has been so, but the two incumbents may still not always see eye-to-eye on everything. For three years, from May 1970 onwards, the Conservatives held sway simultaneously at Westminster and in County Hall; but there was little communication, and consequently little understanding between the wooden and impersonal Edward Heath on the one hand and the hail-fellow-well-met Desmond Plummer on the other. Indeed, their relationship became icy after an incident in Parliament Square, when Heath's car was caught in a nasty traffic snarl-up. Heath decided that Plummer was the man responsible for the traffic jam, and gave orders that he was to be contacted at once. Fortunately or unfortunately, Plummer was attending an international conference of civic leaders in Tokyo at the time, but a call was put through to him in Japan to tell him of Ted Heath's plight and displeasure. Just how Plummer was expected to unsnarl the traffic in Parliament Square from 6,000 miles away was never made clear!

Despite this unpromising background, London Transport was not subjected to any undue political stresses during its first year or two under the aegis of the GLC. Indeed, by 1972 both the Council and the Government were coming to recognise the predominant role played by public transport in getting people to and from their work in the London area, and in moving people within Central London. One reason for this period of comparatively good relations between the Tory politicians and the LT professionals was LT's ability to meet the financial directives laid down by the GLC, without too drastic fares rises and without any serious fall in the total figure of traffic carried by the undertaking. For the first year of the new regime, 1970, the GLC directive required LT to make enough 'profit' on its revenue account to set up a reserve of £2million; in fact, the revenue surplus was £3.7million. For 1971, the GLC required the reserve to be raised to £4million; in fact, the year's operating surplus was only £0.7million, but with the balance bought forward from the previous year, the directive could still be met with a small margin to spare. For 1972, the GLC directive required only a nominal operating surplus, but the actual figure was as much as £2.6million. Of course, all these surpluses were somewhat artificial, owing their existence to the virtual absence of interest charges as a result of the write-off of the undertaking's accumulated capital debt at the end of 1969, and of the grants by the Government and GLC towards LT's capital expenditure (amounting to over £50million of the total investment of £83million over the three years 1970-72).

Although the Conservative administration at County Hall was anxious to see that there was no loss on the LT operating account – and thus no need for any revenue grant – under the new financial regime, it seemed quite willing to put large sums of ratepayers' money into the development and modernisation of the London Transport network. Horace Cutler, then Plummer's deputy and Chairman of the Council's powerful Policy & Resources Committee, with a special interest in transport, claimed in retrospect that the deal with the Government had turned out a bad one, and that up to £100million more should have been paid over by the Government (in addition to the capital write-off) to help with the up-dating of the ageing London Transport system. This may seem a little hard, seeing that after the GLC takeover of LT the Government continued to provide capital grants amounting to some 40% of the undertaking's total investment outlay, and actually increased the range of these grants. For its part, the Tory council weighed in with a useful 21% of the capital requirement, which was rather more than London Transport had expected. Cutler has recorded that when he asked Sir Richard Way, the then LT Chairman, what he needed from the Council in terms of capital funds, Way quoted a figure of £40million; when Cutler agreed at once without demur, Way was clearly astonished and delighted. This enthusiasm for capital grants rather than revenue support for LT was to be found again in the later Conservative administration in County Hall; clearly the Tories preferred to get something tangible for their money.

There were three fares increases in the 1970-72 period to enable London Transport to meet the GLC's financial directives. The first of these took place in August 1970, the second in January 1972 and the third in September 1972. The loss of traffic as a result of these increases seems to have been small; discounting the transfer of the Country Bus & Coach system to the National Bus Co at the end of 1969, the annual London Transport passenger-mileage (the best criterion of demand) fell from 6,725 million in 1969 to 6,666 million in 1972, ie a drop of less than 1%. However, these figures concealed varying trends on the bus and Underground systems, and the effects of other factors besides fares. On the buses alone there was a drop in passenger mileage of as much as 8% over the three years, much of it due to a further growth in car ownership, increased traffic congestion and a continued shortage of bus staff. This fall was offset by an actual increase in the Underground passenger-mileage of 7%, largely attributable to the greater reliability of the rail service and the opening of the new Victoria Line to Victoria in 1969 and on to Brixton in 1971. It is difficult to separate out the effects of the fares increases alone, but they are likely to have been quite small; it must be borne in mind that prices rose generally by nearly 25% between 1969 and 1972, so that the fares increases did not stand out as anything unusual.

The fact that buses are labour-intensive while the Underground is capital-intensive led to a big disparity between the bus and Underground working results under the new financial regime in the early 1970s; the buses made a series of working losses, while the Underground made a series of 'profits' and the question arose whether, under the terms of the 1969 Act, the most unprofitable of the bus services – mostly in the suburbs – should be closed down altogether. It was, however, felt that as the undertaking as a whole was achieving its modified financial targets, there was no call for any general programme of bus network cuts, which might in any case have been contested as illegal under the 'adequate service' provisions of the 1969 Act.

In other ways too the buses were facing intensified problems at this time, while the Underground was riding high. Between 1969 and 1972 the number of buses entering the central area during the morning peak period went down from 4,000 to 3,500, while the number of cars went up from 71,000 to 97,000; the buses were still carrying most of the passengers entering Central London by road, but they were impeded more and more by private cars occupying an inordinate amount of the limited in-town road space in relation to the numbers of their occupants. In 1972 the number of scheduled bus-miles which had to be cut out because of traffic congestion was still running at about the three million mark; compared with a total bus-mileage of 190 million for the year, this may not seem large, but it was no more than the tip of the iceberg in relation to the sum of all bus delays caused by road traffic jams. Although the congestion was at its worst in the central area and its main approaches, it was by no means confined to those parts of London; a number of suburban centres were also severely hit. The Greater London Council and the other traffic authorities were slow in introducing road schemes to give the bus, as the most efficient user of road space, priority over private cars in London. In 1970, for example, there was only a handful of 'bus only' lanes in the London area, while Paris already had over 80. However, there was a gradual acceptance by the GLC and others that such schemes had to come, and by 1972 there were about 40 London bus lanes in operation, with more planned. In addition, the Oxford Street scheme –

involving the closure of that major thoroughfare to all except buses and taxis for a large part of the day – was started, with immediate success.

Apart from traffic congestion, other problems continued to plague the bus operators. Despite improved pay and the introduction of more one-man buses, the shortage of bus staff persisted. At the end of 1972 over 10% of the driver and conductor posts were unfilled and much costly overtime work was needed to keep buses on the road. But in spite of much effort and the stimulus of a new staff bonus related to takings on the buses, no fewer than 14 million bus-miles were lost in that year because of staff shortages. There were problems, too, with the progressive changeover to one-man bus operation, some of them general to bus systems throughout the country, some peculiar to London Transport. The most widespread disadvantage was (and still is) the delay at bus stops while passengers paid their fares to the driver or showed him their travel authority. A Government-sponsored working party on one-man bus operation, which included bus operators and union representatives as well as civil servants from the Transport Ministry, recommended in 1971 greater publicity and more pre-payment of fares, as well as on-the-spot fines for bilkers. To try to overcome boarding delays on its new omo buses, London Transport produced the idea of a 'split' entrance, with one channel for boarding past the driver and the other channel for boarding through an automatic coin-operated gate. There were great difficulties in designing and producing machines which could cope with graduated bus fares and still be rugged enough to stand up to the daily bumping and banging of the average city bus service. LT was to spend large sums of money in perfecting and fitting such machines on omo buses, but the travelling public never took to them and they were very little used. With the later simplification of the fares system and a much greater use of pre-paid tickets and passes, there was eventually little remaining call for these coin-operated gates, and their removal had the added merit of freeing more space in the buses for passengers. LT's earlier omo buses were unpopular in any case, because they involved more standing and congestion in the vehicle. As explained earlier, there was originally a ban on the one-man operation of double-deck buses, and to get its omo bus programme under way, London Transport had to buy large numbers of single-deckers with a high ratio of standing to seated passengers. Naturally, when the ban on double-deck one-man-operation was lifted, LT began buying double-deckers for one-man working. But to introduce omo services as quickly as possible and to qualify for the Government's new bus grants (initially 25%, but upped to 50% in 1971) London Transport was forced to abandon its previous successful policy of designing its own buses, and had to purchase its omo vehicles – single and double-deck – 'off the peg' from standardised designs intended for bus systems throughout the provinces. Predictably, these vehicles did not measure up to the unique conditions of London, with its vast built-up area, where buses have to operate for miles on end through congested city streets. More and more of the omo buses succumbed to mechanical failures, and although the proportion of spare buses was increased, the services suffered badly. At the same time, a national shortage of spare parts began to develop, and there were delays of up to a year in the delivery of some vital bus spares. In the struggle to keep buses on the road, London Transport even had to resort to reconditioning or manufacturing spare parts in its own workshops and garages. One of the few 'plus' items for the London bus operators at this time was the start made with improving the control of buses on the road by installing two-way radio for communication between drivers and controllers and experimenting with bus location systems.

By contrast with the gloomy picture on the bus system, the scene on the

Underground in the early 1970s was a fairly cheerful one. In the year following the opening by the Queen of the main section of the Victoria Line across Central London, the annual rate of users of the new line went up from under 60 million passengers to over 80 million. 1971 saw a spate of new Underground developments. In April of that year work started on the Heathrow Airport extension of the Piccadilly Line, following a ceremony at Hatton Cross in which Sir Desmond (now Lord) Plummer, then GLC Leader, drove an excavator to dig the first load of earth from a working site; report had it that the British Airports Authority – still miffed that the airport's rail link was to be provided by LT rather than BR – insisted that this load of earth should be put back within half an hour of the departure of the notables! In July 1971 the extension of the Victoria Line southwards to its final terminal at Brixton was opened by Princess Alexandra. And in September 1971 work began on the Baker Street-Charing Cross section of the planned Fleet Line (since renamed the Jubilee Line), following a Government announcement that it had authorised a 75% infrastructure grant towards the cost of that stage; the GLC had already agreed to pay the remaining 25%. The Conservatives' belief in capital support rather than operating subsidies was further illustrated in 1971 by the Government's decision to extend the scope of its infrastructure grant scheme to cover 75% of the cost of all urban railway rolling stock and other rail equipment such as signalling. This recognised the need to complement the expansion of the Underground network with a programme for updating and re-equipping the existing system, much of which had been built between the 1860s and 1920s and needed a major face-lift. The updating plan which LT drew up called for an expenditure of £275million over 20 years. The core of the plan was the modernisation of a number of the largest stations, which offered the best chance of improving the public image of the system; it is a striking fact that out of nearly 250 Underground stations, a mere 30 – mostly in and around the central area – account for nearly one half of all station passenger movements (starting or ending journeys, or interchanging between lines) over the whole network. Other efforts to modernise the system and make it more efficient continued. Following the abandonment of coal-firing in LT's main electric power station at Lots Road, the auxiliary generating station at Greenwich was converted to operation by gas turbines, which could be switched on at short notice to help with the peak load. More sections of line were equipped with automatic 'programmed' signalling, centrally supervised, enabling many local signalboxes to be closed and staff saved. There had been problems with the automatic fare collection system introduced with the Victoria Line; the system had proved over-ambitious technically and anyway needed to be applied over the whole network if it was to be really effective. So in 1972 LT decided instead to instal simpler and more reliable inward gates at a large number of stations as quickly as possible; this scheme was meant to claw back most of the money lost by fares evasion at a fraction of the cost of the original plan based on the Victoria Line type installations.

One political frustration for London Transport in the early 1970s arose from its efforts to close the Epping-Ongar line, a rural railway run as a feeder to the Underground, lying wholly outside the GLC area (in Essex), carrying a sparse traffic and losing money quite heavily. After a public inquiry, the Transport Users' Consultative Committee for London reported to the Environment Secretary – with whom the verdict lay – that the closure would cause hardship. The Secretary of State finally decided that the line should stay, but would not give any Government money to meet the losses on the service which he had reprieved! Some years later, London Transport succeeded in persuading Essex Council to help for a time in meeting the losses from the line.

Above:
The 'start of works' ceremony for the tube extension to Heathrow Airport, April 1971. With Sir Desmond Plummer, then GLC Leader, are Sir Richard Way and Horace Cutler. *London Transport*

Below:
The official party at the Heathrow extension 'start of works' ceremony, April 1971. *London Transport*

Left:
Peter Walker, then Transport Minister, visits the Victoria Line extension to Brixton in 1971. With him are Bill Maxwell of LT, and Sir Desmond Plummer. *LT News*

Below:
Moorgate station (Metropolitan Line) before it rebuilding as part of a development scheme in the 1970s. *Ian Allan Library*

The honeymoon period of London Transport's early years under GLC control was disturbed by comparatively few examples of direct County Hall intervention in the affairs of the bus and Underground businesses, most of them concerned with fares. One such case occurred in 1971, when the GLC issued a formal direction to LT to charge children the full adult fare during the peak periods; when London Transport implemented this directive in the morning peaks, there was an outcry, but running the extra buses needed for schoolchildren at the height of the morning peak period was certainly highly uneconomic, and it was in any case open to the education authorities to subsidise school bus services if they so wished. A fares decision in the opposite direction was made by the GLC in 1972, when they turned down a number of the proposals put forward by London Transport in its scheme for a general fares increase; the effect was to limit the rises in bus fares and Underground season ticket rates, and so halve the expected yield from the fares increase. Another initiative on fares came from the London Boroughs, the second tier of local government in London. Under the 1969 Act local authorities were allowed to make arrangements with LT for reduced fares for old age pensioners, so the Boroughs decided to pay LT for letting pensioners travel on the buses outside the peak hours at children's fares.

The Tory GLC seems to have gone into its stewardship of London Transport in 1970 with certain pre-conceived ideas – for example, that LT should at least cover its day-to-day working expenses from the fares that it collected – but otherwise with a reasonably open mind on what should be done with the undertaking which it was taking under its wing. This was shown by the Green Paper entitled 'The Future of London Transport' which the Council put out in 1970 as a consultative document; it was intended to set out the problems of LT and possible solutions, and 'to stimulate discussion and debate . . . with a view to formulating an immediate policy acceptable not only to the Council and the Executive (LT) but also to the users of the service and those who work in it'. This document was discussed at a number of special public meetings organised by the GLC in Central London and the suburbs in the early part of 1971, and the results of the exercise were debated by the Council in full session in July of that year. The outcome was the issue of a series of official directions by the Council to London Transport, of which the most important was probably one which called on the undertaking to fix its fares in such a way that – subject to achievement of the overall financial target – the maximum amount of passenger traffic should be attracted to use the system. This 'value for money' criterion, which had been developed by LT itself, was applicable not only to fixing fare levels but also to deciding for or against new capital and revenue schemes. Other Council directions to London Transport arising from the 'Future of London Transport' document were to do with improving the reliability of the services, simplifying the structure of bus and Underground fares, charging higher fares in the centre than in the suburbs (and on the Underground than on the buses), service closure procedures, and the possibility of introducing minibuses on selected routes.

On one major exercise in this honeymoon period, London Transport worked closely with the Greater London Council. The occasion was the public inquiry into the Greater London Development Plan which the GLC had published at the end of 1969. The inquiry, headed by an eminent QC, Sir Frank Layfield, opened in October 1970, and it was decided that LT should appear before it as part of the GLC team but should be free to submit a separate statement of its views to the inquiry and to provide its own witnesses (of whom the author was one). The London Transport submission stressed the dominant role played by public transport in carrying people to and from their work throughout Greater London, and in handling travellers of all kinds to, from and within the Central area. In practice LT's oral witnesses often

Above:
Oxford Street reserved for buses and taxis, 1973. *London Transport*

Below:
A 'Contraflow' bus lane in Piccadilly, 1972. *London Transport*

appeared before the inquiry at the same time as the GLC's own transport experts, including the wordy Peter Stott (who later moved to the water industry) and the knowledgeable David Bayliss (the Council's Chief Transport Planner).

The surge of support for public transport was given further impetus with the publication in December 1972 of a special report on Urban Transport Planning by the House of Commons Expenditure Committee. This recommended that national policy should be directed towards promoting public transport and discouraging the use of cars for the journey to work in city areas, and that the Environment Department should take a positive line on urban transport, laying down a broad approach which it should ensure that local authorities followed. Other recommendations were that more urban rapid transit railway schemes should be investigated; that local authorities should be made to introduce bus lanes and other traffic management measures to help the bus operators; that a special programme of urban busways should be considered; that parking meter zones should be enlarged to cover the central area and main suburban centres of every big city, with stricter enforcement; that various steps should be taken to cut down the amount of off-street parking in central areas; and that the Department of the Environment should allow for operating grants to public transport as part of the proposed new grant arrangements, provided that they were not used to cover up management inefficiency.

For its part the Greater London Council decided that from the beginning of 1973 it would shoulder another of LT's financial burdens by providing the money which had to be set aside each year for the depreciation and renewal of assets. It will be recalled that the Council had halved the autumn 1972 bus fares increase proposed by London Transport, and was under an obligation to make up the shortfall in yield in the following years in some other way. The scale of this new grant is shown by the fact that LT had put aside over £13½million for depreciation and renewals in 1972. Writing several years later, Sir Horace Cutler said the LT was 'more or less remaining solvent' until 1973, when the Labour party took over the GLC; thereafter the pattern changed to one of deficit and 'that destroyed the financial stability of London Transport for the rest of the decade'. To a large extent, this was true; but it must be noted for the record that the first GLC administration to restrict a fares increase and to authorise a large revenue grant to London Transport was a Tory one. In fact, the depreciation and renewal grant, as it came to be known, was enough not only to make a fares increase in 1973 unnecessary, but even to convert a revenue loss of about £8million in that year into a theoretical surplus of £10million. It may be that the timing of the Conservative GLC's decisions on fares restraint and the revenue grant was influenced by the fact that the Council elections were due to take place in the spring of 1973. If so, whatever hopes the Plummer administration had placed on this factor were dashed, as the Labour party won the 1973 GLC Election with comparative ease.

3
After the Honeymoon

By the time that the Conservatives gave up the reins of office at County Hall in 1973, the relationship between the Council and the London Transport management had already begun to deteriorate. In particular there were differences on how far the Council could go in giving directions to LT on the running of the business, and on the speed with which the Council was introducing measures to give buses priority on the roads. The strains in the GLC-LT relationship were still not severe, but it is doubtful whether the London Transport board would have repeated in 1973 some of the rather rosy statements which it had made in its 1970 Annual Report.

One event which took place while the Tories held sway at County Hall, and which was significant in the light of later wrangles, was the appointment of Ralph Bennett, the ex-Manchester bus manager, as Deputy Chairman and Managing Director (Buses) of LT. This appointment was made in June 1971 on the retirement of the gifted and experienced Anthony Bull from the Vice-Chairmanship. On seniority the bookish Michael Robbins might have expected to take Bull's place as second-in-command of the undertaking; as it was, he had to be content with the overlordship of the Underground system. Bennett's image as a cheerful, successful and down-to-earth bus operator seems to have appealed to Plummer and Cutler, who thought that he would make a good future chairman of London Transport; the doubts were to come later.

The Labour administration which took over at County Hall in May 1973 was headed by the rather grey but earnest figure of Sir Reginald Goodwin. It was during his tenure of office as Leader of the GLC that the division between moderates and militants in the Labour ranks began to become obvious. Sir Reg himself was a Labourite of the old school, and even his opponent Horace Cutler – who by 1974 had succeeded Desmond Plummer as Leader of the GLC Conservative group – was later moved to pay tribute to Goodwin's dedicated record of public service over four decades and to sympathise with him over the stress of living with the militant trends in his party. For the time being, however, the Labour nominees to lead the GLC Transport Committee – Evelyn (later Dame Evelyn) Denington as chairman and the diminutive Jim Daly as vice-chairman – were moderates who, while sympathetic to public transport, nevertheless harboured some suspicions of the largely Tory-appointed LT board.

In July 1973, only two months after the Labour takeover, the Greater London Council came out with a statement of its strategy for promoting public transport and curbing peak-hour car commuting. This was followed in September by the issue of a GLC paper under the title of 'London – The Future and You', in which the Council tried to make it clear that it was not opposed to private motoring as such, but only to the use of cars at peak times in and around Central London and in other congested areas.

Inherent in the Labour Council's pro-LT policy was the avoidance of further fare increases, and in its first year, 1973, it was saved from worry on that score by the 'overkill' effect of the depreciation and renewal grant introduced by its Tory predecessors in the previous year. Another factor was the serious worsening of LT's staff shortage in 1973, which meant that the staff costs for the year were less than had been budgeted for. In terms of the effect on services, this manpower shortage was disastrous. On the buses the shortfall of staff amounted to over 15%, and despite much overtime and rest-day working, the loss of scheduled service was well over 10%. The position on the Underground was even worse; by the end of 1973 the train-miles not operated because of staff shortage had risen to 12% of the full scheduled service. A package of big improvements in wages and conditions, to attract more staff of the calibre needed into the undertaking, was worked out during 1973, but it could not be introduced then – even with the Labour GLC's blessing – because of the Heath Government's incomes legislation. London Transport's manpower problems were especially worrying because of the unattractive working conditions for the operating staff and the difficulty of finding housing for them in the areas where they were most needed. In January 1974 Sir Reg Goodwin saw the Prime Minister, Ted Heath, to discuss the whole problem of manpower shortages, incomes policy, housing and population trends in Greater London, and it is certain that London Transport's special difficulties figured on their agenda. This must however have been Heath's last official involvement in London's affairs; in the following month the Conservatives narrowly lost the General Election, and in March Harold Wilson returned as Prime Minister in a precariously balanced Parliament. He was to consolidate his position in a second General Election in October of the same year, when Labour secured a small working majority in the Commons. These changes meant that for over three years, from March 1974 onwards, Labour ruled simultaneously in the country and in Greater London.

Within a few months of the advent of the new Wilson Government, Stage 3 of the previous Government's Pay Code was ended and London Transport was free, with GLC approval, to bring in its big package of improvements in staff pay and conditions. The results were dramatic; within 18 months, the shortage of bus drivers, for example, was reduced from 22% to under 11%, and there was a marked improvement in the services, both on the buses and the Underground. The reduction in the amount of overtime worked by the staff meant that there was some loss in individual productivity; thus the annual bus-miles per driver/conductor – which had risen steadily from 8,220 in 1967 to 9,580 in 1973 (largely as a result of the switch to one-man operations on many routes) – fell back again to under 9,000 in 1975.

Also, of course, the cost of the big improvements in pay and conditions, and the rise in total staff as a result of them, added enormously to London Transport's wages bill. The fuel bill, too, was rising astronomically because of the sudden increase in oil prices; by February 1974, for example, the cost of the oil fuel used in London Transport's power stations had risen fourfold in nine months, and LT was planning to switch to natural gas to generate the electricity that it needed. Overall, the undertaking's working expenses went up by a massive £45million (over 27%) between 1973 and 1974, and a frightening £99million (47%) between 1974 and 1975. Admittedly, inflation generally in Britain 'took off' in the initial years of the Labour Government, with the retail price index rising by 16% in 1974 and over 24% in 1975; but LT's costs outstripped even these appalling figures.

Thanks to the Council's fares freeze policy, and despite the continuing effects of the staff shortage, the number of passengers carried by London Transport went up in 1973 and again in 1974. As we have seen, the new depreciation and renewal grant introduced by the Tories kept London Transport nominally solvent through 1973 and even provided a somewhat spurious surplus of £10million to be carried forward

Above:
A bus driver recruitment poster of the 1970s.
London Transport

into 1974. But even that surplus, plus a depreciation grant of nearly £20million and the small extra revenue from additional traffic, was not enough to offset the big rise in working expenses in 1974. Pledged to keep London Transport fares frozen, the Labour GLC was in that year forced to start direct deficit financing of the undertaking, the sum supplied to bridge the gap – nearly £24million – being dubbed fares relief grant.

Foreseeing the even worse rise in costs in 1975, the board of London Transport kept up unwelcome pressure on the Council (and through it on the Government also) for a clear and firm decision on future fares policy. It was stressed that even if the fares freeze was maintained, the financial support given to London Transport by the Council and the Government was still likely to be – in percentage terms – well below that received by public transport operators in most great cities abroad. On the other hand, the rise in LT costs was exceptionally severe, and if the Council was going to get cold feet and end the fares freeze anyway, it would be best for all concerned if the fares increases came sooner rather than later, and were the result of planning rather than panic.

Late in 1974 the GLC decided that in view of LT's expected enormous increase in working costs in 1975, the fares freeze would have to end, and fares would go up by over 30% early in the new year. The new fares, based on simplified scales, were duly introduced in March, but their yield still fell well short of the total expected deficit. The Council was still trying to establish a longer-term basis for financing London Transport's rocketing costs, and in mid-1975 came up with a formula whereby the fares relief grant would be pegged – in real terms – to its 1975 level, and fares would be raised as need be to cover the rest of the estimated shortfall. To get this formula into operation, another fares increase was required, so in November 1975 fare levels rose by another 25% or more. But even so, the Council was still faced with paying out fares relief grant of no less than £93million for the year.

When 1975 began there had been no fares increase on the buses for three years and none of the Underground system for over two years. Against a background of rising inflation this meant that the travelling public of London had been enjoying a progressive reduction in the real price of their journeys, at the expense of the ratepayers. Then suddenly, in a belated attempt to claw back some of the growing losses, the fares were raised by a total of over 60% in the one year, 1975. This was the second big see-sawing of LT fares resulting mainly from the differing transport philosophies of the two main political parties; unfortunately it was not to be the last.

It was, incidentally, not only the Labour GLC which had got cold feet at the size of the operating subsidies to which its fares freeze policy had led. A circular issued by the Labour Government at the end of 1974 on rates support throughout the country and the new system of Transport Supplementary Grant (TSG) said that it was the Government's aim that bus services generally should move a lot nearer to paying their way on a commercial basis. Rises in fares, said the circular, should at least match increases in costs, and where fares had not been keeping pace with costs, higher rises still would be needed.

The Transport Supplementary Grant system was an attempt by the Government to use its financial support for highways and public transport to achieve what it thought to be the right balance between private and public means of travel. The new TSG was to replace a number of separate Government grants for road construction and maintenance and for public transport (for example, infrastructure grants); it was to be paid through the GLC and county authorities after the Government had received and considered each year a statement of every authority's proposed expenditure – capital and revenue – on highways and on public transport support.

An Underground staff recruitment poster of the 1970s. *London Transport*

These statements were to be known as Transport Policies and Programmes (TPPs) and would reveal whether a particular county was – in the Government's view – unduly favouring one mode of transport or the other, or simply proposing too much expenditure on transport generally; the amount of TSG finally paid out would depend on an authority's willingness to conform to the Government's ideas.

From 1975, as a result of the new system, part of the GLC's grant to London Transport to meet the annual operating deficit was repaid to the Council in the form of Transport Supplementary Grant.

Sir Horace Cutler was critical of LT's costly 1974 deal with the unions, on the grounds that the unions offered nothing in the way of increased productivity in return for the big improvements in their members' pay and conditions. Given the circumstances of the time, this criticism seems rather misplaced. There was then fierce competition for staff of the right calibre in the London area, and LT – with its unattractive working hours and shift system – was woefully short of suitable bus and Underground workers. In any case, the programme which had offered the best productivity prospects – the conversion of the bus system to one-man bus operation – was slowing down, not because of union resistance but because the delays created by passengers boarding omo buses on heavily-used routes in congested areas were proving prohibitive. So the single-manning programme, which had raised the number of one-man-operated LT buses from a scheduled figure of just over 500 at the start of 1970 to more than 2,100 (nearly 40% of the total service fleet) at the end of 1973, made little headway from 1974 onwards. This frustrating loss of impetus was in stark contrast with LT's earlier confident assertion that the whole London bus fleet would be converted to one-man-operation by the end of the 1970s.

There were other frustrations, too, for London's busmen in the middle 1970s. Many unsatisfactory single-deck buses, bought 'off the peg' to qualify for Government bus grant and get the omo programme moving, had to be withdrawn from service before completing their expected life-span. Late deliveries of new buses and a nationwide shortage of spare parts meant that the number of serviceable buses fell seriously short of the demand. Hopes of introducing a new network of limited-stop Speedbus services on trunk routes were dashed when the Greater London Council decided that it could not guarantee the proposed services the special traffic priorities which they needed to succeed. Experiments with new types of local bus service – carried out partly in response to pressure from the earlier Tory GLC, and using minibuses (and in one case 'dial-a-bus' operation) – were mostly unsuccessful and had to be modified to survive as regular services. A sudden petrol famine early in December 1973 took many private cars temporarily off the road and so produced, while it lasted, a dramatic cut of 50% in the amount of bus mileage lost through traffic congestion; but despite this demonstration of the effect of too many cars on city street, the GLC was still unable to introduce all the schemes for bus priority and restrictions on car usage in congested areas that it and London Transport would have liked.

One interesting change brought about by the Greater London Council soon after the Labour takeover in 1973 was the replacement of the cheap bus fare scheme for the elderly by free off-peak bus travel for all Greater London residents of pensionalble age. Altogether about one million elderly Londoners took advantage of the new scheme, and there was a big rise in the number of journeys that they made. Unfortunately London Transport gained nothing from this extra traffic; the compensation paid by the Council to LT did not cover it. Indeed, the undertaking was often actually worse off; organised parties of pensioners would sometimes fill a sequence of buses and crowd out the fare-paying passengers. Regrettably, some

HIGH FIDELITY
FINCHLEY ROAD
268 Hampstead Village
Swiss Cottage
OHX 443E
VLW 145G

LONDON TRANSPORT

Left:
An early one-man-operated single-deck bus in Hampstead. *London Transport*

Below:
Prematurely-discarded single-deck buses awaiting disposal at Radlett Aerodrome, 1975. *Capital Transport*

London pensioners have now come to regard their free travel on LT services as a right rather than a concession paid for by their fellow-Londoners, and a case could be made out for asking pensioners to make some token contribution, however small, towards the cost of their journeys.

For the Underground, the middle 1970s were years of mixed fortunes. Work went forward on building the tube extension to Heathrow Airport and the first section of the Fleet (now Jubilee) Line; but the Government resisted pressure to authorise the trunk section of the Fleet Line from Charing Cross to Fenchurch Street, and a London Transport report in the autumn of 1973 on the possibility of revitalising and redeveloping the Docklands area of Southeast London on the back of the Fleet Line project was not received with any marked enthusiasm. Encouraged by its experience with one-man train operation on the Victoria Line, the LT management started installing extra equipment to enable trains on the Hammersmith and City and Circle services to be operated manually by one man; but it undertook the work before the union had fully agreed the terms on which its members would accept one-manning on these trains, with the result that the latter were still being operated with two-man crews 10 years later.

Other developments on the Underground in the mid-1970s included the further spread of the simplified automatic fare collection system at stations (concentrating on making sure that all passengers had a ticket before starting their journeys), and

Below:
New Underground lines since 1965. *R. Armstrong*

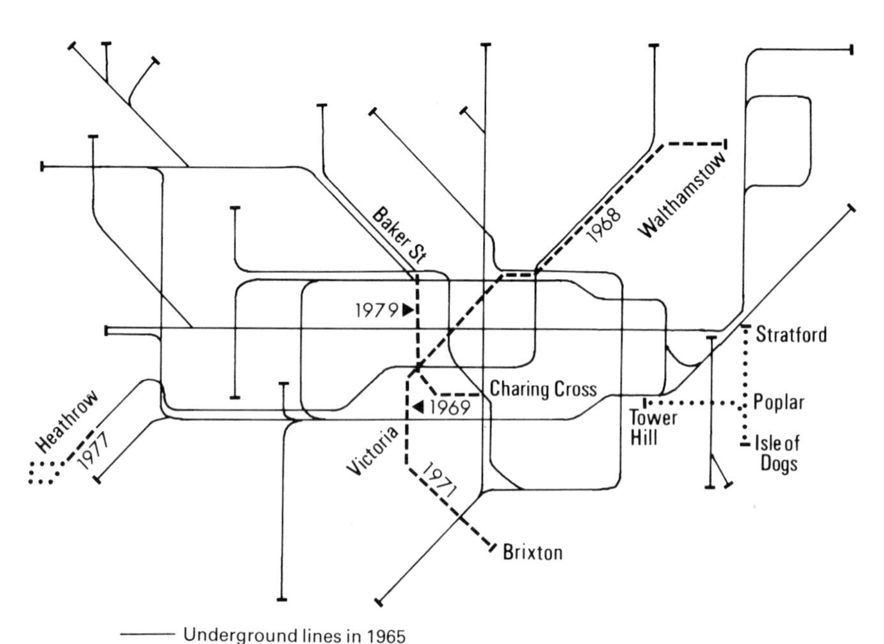

the further expansion of car parks at suburban stations, with special financial help from the GLC.

Also, in this period, the Government and the GLC got together with the two big public transport operators in the London area – London Transport and British Railways – to carry out an intensive review of the whole railway network in and around London, known as the London Rail Study. The Study Team, to which the author belonged, was asked to investigate the existing condition of London's railways, identify its main problems, see how expected changes in London and the Southeast would affect the demand on the rail network, decide what options were open to adapt the system to the changing needs, and assess the merits and demerits of those options. The Study was commissioned early in 1973, under Conservative auspices, and its results were published in two stages in late 1974 and early 1975, under Labour auspices. The Study was probably the most far-reaching review of London's railways ever produced, and is still valuable as a basic work of reference on the London rail system. The Study report stressed the need for adequate staffing of the system, and presented three alternative capital investment strategies for the remaining quarter of the 20th century, ranging in cost from £2,000million to £2,400million. Both these figures included no less than £1,400million for first priority works, ie the renewals essential simply to keep the existing system going. Varying sums were suggested for the second priority programme, covering improvements to the existing system, and for the third priority category, covering actual expansion of the network. The report recommended that an early start should be made on the important second stage of the Fleet Line, and that the line should eventually be extended eastwards through Docklands to Woolwich and Thamesmead. It also recommended – though with a lower priority – a new tube line from the southwest to the northeast, dubbed the 'Chelsea-Hackney line'.

The Rail Study report clearly favoured capital subsidies in preference to fares subsidies; it also came out against flat fares on London's rail system, and concluded that even a zonal fares system would not work under London conditions – a conclusion that was to be proved wrong on the Underground in the 1980s. On the question of organisation, the Study report suggested that the four bodies which had sponsored the Study itself should together set up a permanent rail advisory committee for London, which would put forward agreed plans for rail investment and fares, and so avoid as far as possible any clashes between the different political authorities controlling London Transport and British Railways.

As with so many official inquiries and reviews, much of what the London Rail Study proposed was ignored; but the Study report remains as a full and generally sound analysis of London's railways as they approached the last quarter of the 20th century.

The end of 1974 and start of 1975 saw a change in the top personality of London Transport. Sir Richard Way, who had fought so doughtily for LT through a difficult period of political 'stop-go' in the GLC, departed to become Principal of King's College, London. It may be surmised that neither Sir Richard nor the Council had any great regrets at this parting of the ways; at the formal lunch given by the GLC's black Chairman, Lord Pitt, for Sir Richard on his departure, the speeches were none too cordial and were delivered largely tongue-in-cheek. Sir Richard left, in his own words, 'to make way for an older man'. The new incumbent, Kenneth (now Sir Kenneth) Robinson, was already 64 when he took over at 55 Broadway. He came from a background of business and politics, having been a company secretary before becoming Minister of Health and then Minister for Planning & Land under

Left:
Sir Kenneth Robinson, Chairman of LT 1975-78. *London Transport*

Below:
The author (left) with Kenneth Robinson, LT Chairman, at a reception in 1975. *Author*

Harold Wilson in the 1960s. When the Labour Government fell in 1970, Robinson took on the staff management job in the British Steel Corporation, and it was from there that he moved to LT. Robinson combined strength of character with a kindly personality and a lively interest in the arts – an interest which was later to lead to his chairmanship of the Arts Council.

In view of the inferiority complex that Sir Richard Way had inspired in the GLC politicians, it was perhaps rather surprising that they should have chosen another figure from the national rather than the local scene as his successor. It may be that the Labour members of the Council expected Robinson, as a fellow-member of the party, to take London Transport wherever they wanted it to go. If so, they were sorely disappointed; Kenneth Robinson ran his new job without political bias, and stood up for the professional independence and integrity of the undertaking just as firmly as his predecessor had done. He was in any case clearly saddened by the growing militant trend in the Labour Party, and it came as no surprise later, when the SDP was formed, that he should be among the first to transfer his allegiance to it.

The new Chairman was to be sorely tested within a mere two months of taking up his appointment. On 28 February 1975 London Transport suffered the worst disaster in the history of the undertaking, when – for no discoverable reason – a tube train was driven into a dead-end tunnel at Moorgate and 43 people (including the driver) lost their lives. Kenneth Robinson met the test well, helping the victims' families, leading LT mourners at memorial services in St Paul's Cathedral and locally, and pressing for any further practical steps towards eliminating accidents on the Underground.

For other reasons, too, 1975 was a testing year for the new LT Chairman. As we have already seen, the GLC's change of mind on fares took effect in that year, and there were two fares rises totalling over 60%. Of course, passengers had been paying less and less in real terms while the preceding fares freeze had lasted, so that the increases were to some extent a catching-up process; also, inflation was rampant, reaching a record figure of over 24% in 1975, so that the size of the fare rises was less obvious to the public. In addition, the cut in the manpower shortage meant that bus and Underground services improved markedly. The net result was a much smaller drop in traffic (just over 4%) than might have been expected from the big fare increases alone. But 1975 was still not an easy year for a newcomer to the business.

Nor was the following year much better. Although staffing continued to improve and more bus and train mileage was operated, the amount of fares relief grant was cut, and fares had to be raised by no less than 25% in mid-1976. This was well in excess of the rate of inflation for the year, and resulted in a drop of over 5% in the annual passenger-mileage, mostly on the Underground.

The cut in fares relief grant was due to a corresponding reduction in the Transport Supplementary Grant paid to the GLC by the Government. This reduction was ordered in spite of the Labour Government's previous commitment to a whole-hearted support of public transport in London (as shown by its endorsement of the final version of the Greater London Development Plan, which stressed the vital role that public transport had to play in making London 'a prosperous and pleasant place in which to live'). But Callaghan, who had taken over from Harold Wilson as Prime Minister in the spring of 1976, saw that something had to be done to bring down the murderous level of inflation, and London Transport was one of the victims of the Labour Government's corrective measures. The change in the Government's attitude was also shown by a new consultation document on transport policy which it put out during 1976, and which was criticised by London Transport for failing to recognise the importance of public transport as an alternative to the car in busy town and city centres. LT pointed out that reduced Government support meant a higher level of fares, which could drive more workers out of Central London and possibly out of the London area altogether. It might have added that the alternative of making the ratepayer contribute more could have much the same effect, since firms were already pulling out of London because of their high rate and rent bills.

Sadly, it looked as if the cuts in grant were going to be extended to capital investment as well. London Transport's capital programme for 1977, already modest, was cut by £10million. This meant that, apart from expenditure on the first stage of the Jubilee Line and on the Heathrow Extension, nearly all the money invested in the undertaking in that year would have to be used merely in repairing and replacing existing property and equipment. Little wonder that the London Transport management looked enviously across the Channel to its counterparts in the Paris Transport Authority, on whom the French Government was lavishing funds, aimed at turning the Paris system into a first-rate public service and a valuable international showcase for French technology.

Above:
The Moorgate disaster, 1975. Clearing the tunnel. *LT News*

4 Horace Cutler in Command

As it turned out, 1977 was to bring London Transport more hope on the capital front, as Labour was defeated in the GLC Spring election of that year and a Tory administration took over the reins again in County Hall. The new Leader of the Council was the swashbuckling and publicity-seeking Horace Cutler, the urbane Desmond Plummer having in the meantime quitted politics to take on the doubtless more congenial job of chairing the Horserace Betting Levy Board. In its attitude to the London Transport business, the new Council took much the same line as the earlier Conservative regime under Plummer had done, favouring development expenditure – especially on profitable projects – at the expense of revenue grants.

Not unexpectedly therefore, LT fares were raised again in July 1977 by 15%, but the Silver Jubilee brought millions more visitors to London during the year, so that the total figure of passenger-mileage on the bus and Underground networks was only very marginally down on that for 1976.

At the end of 1977 London Transport got a much-needed boost to its morale from the opening of the Underground extension to the heart of Heathrow Airport. This was billed as the world's first direct link between a major international airport and the underground railway system of a capital city, and the importance of the occasion was shown by the presence of the Queen to perform the opening ceremony. In the very first week after the opening, up to 24,000 passengers a day were being carried to and from the centre of the airport by the new line.

Another sign of hope came with the publication of a Government White Paper on transport policy during 1977. Although this did not go as far as LT would have liked in recognising the essential rôle of public transport in keeping cities working, it did show that the Government had taken on board many of the criticisms that had been made of its earlier consultation paper. In particular the Government said that instead of halving its financial help for public transport within five years, as it had previously intended, it now proposed to maintain its aid at the existing levels.

On the other hand, the Government turned down a recommendation in a report of the Select Committee on Nationalised Industries during 1977 for the Greater London Council to be named the Passenger Transport Authority for the Greater London area, with London Transport as the Passenger Transport Executive. With this status, the GLC and LT would have had a say in the financing and passenger services of British Railways in the London area, on a similar basis to that established in the other Metropolitan Counties. The recommendation was made because the Select Committee considered it the best way of achieving real co-ordination of all forms of public transport in London. Although a rail advisory committee for London had been set up to improve BR-LT co-ordination, following the earlier London Rail Study, the differing political and financial policies imposed on the two undertakings by the Government and GLC were still making real integration difficult. The basic reason why the Callaghan administration turned down the Select Committee's proposal was doubtless political; a Labour Government was hardly likely to welcome

Above:
The opening of the Heathrow extension, 1977: the Queen with Kenneth Robinson at Hatton Cross station. *London Transport*

Left:
The opening of the Heathrow extension, 1977: the Queen with Graeme Bruce of LT (left) in the cab of the inaugural train. *London Transport*

legalised intervention by a Tory GLC in British Rail's passenger operations in London. But the proposal was probably inadequate anyway, since much of the BR suburban network radiating from London lies outside the Greater London boundaries, and would not have been covered by the new scheme.

If the Government's rejection of the Select Committee's proposal disappointed Horace Cutler, there was nothing that he could do about it. But there was something that he could do about changing the chairman of London Transport. Cutler has said that when his party won the GLC elections in 1977, he was determined that Kenneth Robinson should go, on the grounds that a politician was not the right man to run a commercial undertaking. In fact Robinson had carefully eschewed politics since leaving the Wilson Government in 1969, and had more than 20 years of commercial experience behind him. But he and Cutler had crossed swords some years earlier, when Robinson had been the Labour Minister of Planning & Land, and Cutler the Tory GLC Housing Committee chairman. So, one way and another, there was little prospect of any real collaboration between the two men in their new relationship. Eventually terms were agreed for Kenneth Robinson to step down from the LT Chairmanship; this he did in March 1978, although he remained as a non-executive member of the LT board until his original four-year contract ran out at the end of that year.

Waiting hopefully in the wings, ready to take on the chairmanship, was Ralph Bennett, who had been second-in-command both to Robinson and to Robinson's predecessor, Sir Richard Way. Cutler had had a hand in appointing Bennett to the deputy chairmanship back in 1971, with a view to his eventual elevation to the top LT job; but later experiences had made Cutler begin to doubt whether Bennett would make an effective chairman after all. However, as Cutler has recorded, he was under strong pressure – from his Tory colleagues in the GLC, from Sir James Swaffield (the Council's Director-General), and from past LT Chairmen – to award Bennett the job. He finally gave in to these pleadings, and Bennett was appointed Chairman for a period of five years from April 1978.

Political control of London Transport under the Cutler administration at County Hall was exercised through three bodies of elected council members. Specific responsibility for LT matters rested with the London Transport Committee, initially chaired by Harold Mote. This reported to the Planning & Communications Policy Committee, presided over by the redoubtable and efficient Shelagh Roberts (later to become a Euro-MP). This in turn reported to the Council itself, under Cutler's leadership. Harold Mote had shown great acumen in his own business, which he had built up from small beginnings after World War 2 to become a thriving concern; but in his dealings with public transport in London he displayed many of the failings of the over-enthusiastic amateur. The first fruits of his efforts were contained in a policy document entitled 'London Transport – A New Look' which the Council made public in October 1977. After London Transport had reacted in dismay to some of the wilder propositions put forward in the paper, the Council backed down to the extent of submitting the controversial document to a process of formal consultation with LT. This embarrassing interlude was largely forgotten when, in the spring of 1978, Harold Mote was elected Chairman (in effect, the Speaker) of the GLC. Personally pleasant and likeable, Mote had nevertheless dreamed up some unpromising schemes for London Transport, including one for a highly convoluted Underground line in west and southwest London, widely known in 55 Broadway as the 'Hairpin Line'.

After Harold Mote's year as GLC Chairman, and the disappearance from public life of Dr Gordon Taylor (who had ably chaired the Council's LT Committee during

Left:
Ralph Bennett, Chairman of LT 1978-80. *London Transport*

Below:
At the start of trial borings for the abortive Stage 3 of the Jubilee Line. Behind the map are Ralph Bennett and Michael Robbins of LT, with Shelagh Roberts (GLC): at the extreme right is Harold Mote. *LT News*

Above:
Horace Cutler opens Stonebridge Park depot, Bakerloo Line in 1979. *LT News*

Left:
Horace Cutler and Ralph Bennett at the Stonebridge Park depot opening in 1979. *LT News*

Mote's absence), he returned to preside over the Committee for the remainder of the Cutler administration's term of office.

The appointment of Ralph Bennett as Chairman of London Transport in the spring of 1978 and Harold Mote's almost simultaneous move from the chair of the Council's LT Committee might have been expected to improve the somewhat sour relationship that had developed between the GLC and London Transport. Unfortunately these changes did nothing of the kind. LT was under formal direction from the Council to hold its fare increases to the prevailing level of inflation and make no significant reduction in services, and to meet any resulting gap between income and expenditure by 'economies in operating costs and increases in productivity supported by capital investment'. Although the management had produced plans to meet this order, including in particular a new 'Bus Plan' designed to match the services more closely to the staff and buses available, it was unable to make these plans work fully, and Ralph Bennett found himself under repeated attack from Cutler for failing to 'deliver the goods'. The atmosphere between the two men was not improved by an incident resulting from the security measures then in force in London Transport – as in many other businesses – against IRA terrorism. Horace Cutler arrived in the lobby at LT headquarters, on his way to a private lunch with Ralph Bennett, who had omitted to have Cutler met and escorted to his room. So Cutler was stopped by the security guard, who did not recognise him. Instead of commending the guard for his vigilance and asking for a message to be sent up to Bennett, Cutler stormed back across the river in a huff.

The personal frictions between the Council Leader and LT Chairman were doubtless exacerbated, on Cutler's side, by his growing conviction that he had made a mistake in yielding to pressure and appointing Bennett to the top LT job. The consequences for London Transport in the next few years were to be traumatic.

5
The Axeman Cometh – and Goeth

During 1978 Horace Cutler made two appointments to the board of London Transport which he hoped would show that the GLC was grappling with the problems of what he called 'an albatross round the necks of the capital's ratepayers'. In the event neither appointment was to produce much benefit to the Londoner or much kudos for Cutler and the Council. One of them, indeed, was to backfire badly.

The first, and less controversial, of the two appointments was that of John Stansby as Deputy Chairman of LT for a period of two years. Stansby was a personal acquaintance of Cutler and ran his own business management firm, from which he was seconded to London Transport. Cutler's idea in appointing him was that, if and when outside consultants had to be brought in to investigate the affairs of LT, Stansby would act as the catalyst. After his appointment, Stansby did in fact get the board to commission an intensive study of its activities by a well-known consultancy concern, PA International. However, much of Stansby's time in London Transport was taken up in master-minding an extensive internal reorganisation which was supposed to decentralise authority and make the undertaking more responsive to its customers' needs and wishes. As a personality, Stansby made no great impact on London Transport, and despite the build-up which preceded his arrival at 55 Broadway, he showed no signs of setting the Thames on fire. It seems clear from Horace Cutler's lively political testament (*The Cutler Files*) that Stansby proved a disappointment to the GLC Leader; there was certainly little regret at his departure from the LT scene in 1980.

Cutler's second appointee to the London Transport board was a different kettle of fish. This was the rebel civil servant, Leslie Chapman, author of the book *Your Disobedient Servant* which the *Daily Express* had described as a 'devasting exposure of bureaucratic extravagance'. In mid-1978, after reading the book, Cutler – in a typically melodramatic gesture – sent Chapman a telegram, care of his publishers, reading 'Must see you urgently about matter of great importance'. The two men met a few days later, when Cutler offered Chapman the London Transport appointment. Chapman's first reaction was to turn the offer down, but he agreed to go away and think it over, and subsequently let Cutler know that he was prepared to take the job on, albeit on a strictly part-time basis.

The announcement of Chapman's appointment – which was to run for two years from the beginning of 1979 – was not made until 2 November 1978. For the media, it was the start of a saga which was to provide them with a source of sensational material, on and off, for a considerable time to come. The appointment was greeted in the London *Evening Standard* with the headline 'London Sends for the Axeman', flanked by a photograph of a smiling Leslie Chapman on his Welsh farm, brandishing a large axe. Perhaps Chapman would have got further with London Transport if this kind of naive public display had been abjured. As it was, the LT management was put on the defensive before Chapman even crossed the threshold of 55 Broadway, and its subsequent reception of his ideas, however sound, was inevitably prejudiced by this unfortunate initial publicity.

During November 1978, Chapman had a meeting with Ralph Bennett, the LT Chairman, who asked him whether he would take on an investigation of building maintenance in London Transport – a field appropriate to Chapman's experience and one which offered much scope for economy and improvement. Apparently suspicious that the suggestion was meant to divert his energies away from LT's wider problems, Chapman turned the job down, saying that it would in any case demand more of his time than he was prepared to give. He also declined to accept the annual fee to which part-time board members were entitled, thus avoiding the possible accusation of 'taking the firm's money' if he wanted to air his views on any of LT's shortcomings.

It is perhaps regrettable that Chapman did not take on the building maintenance investigation in London Transport. It was one of the sectors which was to figure prominently in his later strictures on LT. A thorough investigation into building maintenance would not have prevented him from roaming over wider fields at the same time. As to the amount of effort involved, Chapman was later to offer to work full-time without pay for some months while a cost-cutting unit was being set up. Moreover, when he was advising another authority, Berkshire County Council, he appeared to go along with a sector-by-sector approach to cost-cutting.

The first few LT board meetings that Chapman attended, and the information that he picked up in the early months of 1979, quickly convinced him that there was scope for the exercise of his cost-cutting talents in LT. It is not proposed to reproduce here in detail all of Chapman's accusations against the board nor to set out a complete blow-by-blow account of his differences with LT and eventually with Cutler; these are described in extenso in his second book, *Waste Away*, published in 1982. Suffice it to say that by May 1979 Chapman had come to the conclusion that the board was far too complacent, and had demanded that action be taken to cut expenses. As examples of waste he cited extravagance in the special dining facilities which the board members and senior managers enjoyed, the use of a fleet of large cars (many of them chauffeured) by top executives, the provision of a staff library which duplicated the local lending libraries, over-large offices for board members and their personal staffs, the growth in the number of managers and administrators, the use of excessive manpower in building and civil engineering work (attributable to the employment of direct labour instead of outside designers and contractors), and general inefficiency in the main LT workshops. For some of these items Chapman was able to give chapter and verse; for others, he could only make his own subjective judgment of the extent of the waste involved. Although he could not resist the occasional personal dig at the LT management – as for example when he said that their use of LT cars showed that they found their own product unacceptable – Leslie Chapman appears to have made his accusations on the basis of genuine conviction. Whether or not Horace Cutler had quite the same objectives as Chapman, he later took up some of Chapman's more telling points and used them as ammunition against the LT management. In *The Cutler Files*, for example, he said that 55 Broadway was known as the 'most affluent luncheon club in London' – a description which comes oddly from the former leader of a Council which could scarcely be called frugal in its hospitality and which until quite recently, under Conservative and Labour administrations alike, held regular annual receptions at County Hall, attended by hundreds of local politicians and officials, who were lavishly wined and dined while the great building blazed with light. Again, in *The Cutler Files*, he condemned the use of staff cars by the LT management with the remark that 'obviously people running the buses knew they were too inefficient to risk using them themselves'; yet, elsewhere in the same book, Cutler justified the

Right:
The axeman cometh. Leslie Chapman after the announcement of his LT Board appointment, 1978. *BBC Hulton Picture Library*

Below:
The Jubilee Line opening in 1979: Ralph Bennett, LT Chairman (left) looks on as the Prince of Wales stoops over a dropped card. In the background Horace Cutler gestures dramatically. *London Transport*

use of chauffeur-driven staff cars for himself and the rest of the GLC top brass with the remark that 'it does not make for better government for the Leader of the GLC to stand in a bus queue or strap-hang on the tube'. Clearly, so far as Sir Horace was concerned, what was sauce for the goose was not necessarily sauce for the gander!

It is interesting to note that both Cutler and Chapman considered London Transport to have been well managed before and just after the war. Cutler said that 'London Transport was very well managed in 1950, and not only that, it was an organisation with very high morale'. Chapman said that 'in the 1930s the LPTB was considered to be an efficient and thoroughly up-to-date organisation providing a good service at reasonable cost'. Yet many of the accusations made against LT in recent years could equally have been made in the 1930s and 1950s; then, as later, London Transport board members and senior managers enjoyed their own dining facilities, occupied large offices and used chauffeur-driven staff cars. In practice, the quality of management was probably no better then than it is now – indeed, on occasions it seems to have been rather worse; but the managements of those times were batting on much easier wickets, with more money and a younger system, and their shortcomings were not exposed.

In May 1979 the LT Chairman issued a policy document setting out his ideas on the way forward for the undertaking. A few weeks later Leslie Chapman produced a riposte under the title 'London Transport's Failure to Carry out its Functions Satisfactorily'. Both these documents were circulated inside LT management. The Chapman document drew attention to the undertaking's parlous financial state and prospects, to a recent report by one of the senior LT civil engineers indicating widespread waste in the engineering departments, to the need for productivity measures – with, or if necessary without, the co-operation of the trade unions – and to the desirability of setting up a powerful cost-cutting unit within the undertaking as soon as possible. As Chapman saw it, there were two courses that London Transport could adopt – to cut down everything to the bare essentials and keep the system ticking over at its existing level of service with a minimal management and administrative staff, and no frills; or to rise to the challenges of traffic congestion, inner city decay, high wages and labour problems, and seize every opportunity offered by new technology and the energy crisis. Chapman concluded his report by characterising the LT management grades as conscientious but unimaginative, and called for fresh thinking and a real attempt by the board to meet its management responsibilities.

While the board was recovering from this broadside, Chapman was doing more homework on comparative statistics, and was able to show that despite the large-scale introduction of one-man-operated buses in the 1970s, the bus-miles operated per bus employee – which had gone up by 4% between 1970 and 1973 – had fallen back again by 8% by 1977. As we have seen, this reverse was largely due to the generous package of concessions on working hours and holidays which was granted to the staff, rightly or wrongly, in 1974. In his comparison of London Transport with its counterparts in large cities overseas, Chapman was on weaker ground. The index which he used – passenger journeys per employee – was a misleading one, since it took no account of the average length of journey, which was (and still is) considerably higher in London than in most foreign cities; if the truer index – passenger-miles per employee – had been used, the comparison would have looked a lot better for London Transport.

There was a lull until October 1979, when Ralph Bennett had a private meeting with Chapman, at which the setting-up of a high-level cost-cutting unit in London Transport was agreed. It was at this stage that Chapman offered to work full-time, without pay, for some months – and thereafter as required – to build the unit up and get it into action. However, when the creation of this Central Productivity Unit was duly announced by LT later in October, Chapman was incensed by the fact that he was not asked to master-mind it; while he would be able to advise the unit on how it should function, it was to be directed by full-time LT officials who could reject his advice if they wished.

Chapman now decided that he was getting nowhere within London Transport and that the time had come for him to take his accusations and views to those who had appointed him, the GLC. In November 1979 he wrote two letters. The first, addressed to Ralph Bennett, set out his criticisms of the LT bureaucracy, branded certain items of waste as 'disgraceful', estimated that LT's costs could be cut by between £25million and £50million a year without reducing service levels, gave his reasons for thinking that the organisation of the new Productivity Unit was ill-conceived, and announced his intention of taking the whole controversy outside London Transport in whatever ways seemed to him 'appropriate to serve the public interest'.

Presumably to protect his position, Bennett sent copies of Chapman's letter to Cutler and to Sir James Swaffield, Director-General (Town Clerk) of the GLC. When the contents of the letter came out, Cutler blamed the leak on his own Council's bureaucratic set-up, which he compared with a sink-waste disposal machine – 'anything that goes in comes out in little pieces'.

Chapman's second letter of November 1979 was to Dr Gordon Taylor, Chairman of the GLC Transport Committee. In it he again recounted all his troubles with London Transport, dwelling especially on the increase in the number of managers and the lavishness of the office, dining and staff car facilities available to senior LT officers (which he illustrated with figures of cost).

There followed a telephone conversation between Chapman and Gordon Taylor which, according to the record which Chapman kept of it, included some revealing comments by the GLC transport spokesman. Among other things, Taylor was quoted as saying that, as far as he could make out, Horace Cutler was holding his fire on the Chapman allegations because he did not have enough hard evidence and because he wanted to wait until nearer the Council elections 'for a bit of LT-bashing kudos'. There was also the fear that the GLC Conservatives might attract some of the blame for what was happening in London Transport, since the LT board was composed largely of their nominees.

These considerations did not, however, prevent Horace Cutler from castigating the London Transport management in a letter – leaked to the press – which he sent to Bennett on 14 November 1979, dealing with the rejection of the board's budget proposals for 1980. After recalling that Bennett had asked in 1978 for the relaxation of financial stringency and a year's sabbatical to get things done, the letter went on:

'You have had both. Since then the promised improvements have not materialised; and the budget submissions hold no hope for the future.

'The problem boils down to management, its lack and its quality . . . If the present personnel are unable to manage, then we must find some who can.'

After a stormy meeting of the board at the beginning of December, at which Leslie Chapman's allegations of massive waste in London Transport were rebutted by his colleagues, Chapman wrote direct to Cutler to say that unless LT changed its policies and the organisation of its cost-cutting unit, or alternatively agreed to an independent inquiry, he would be tendering his resignation to the Council.

This ultimatum, and 'revelations' in the London evening papers based on the more sensational parts of the leaked letters from Chapman to Bennett and Gordon Taylor, forced Cutler to take some action. Still in December 1979, London Transport's own auditors – Deloitte, Haskins & Sells – were instructed to investigate Chapman's accusations that LT's waste in various fields put the undertaking in breach of its statutory duty.

The auditors' report was called by for the end of January 1980, and this time limit made it impossible for Deloittes to go into Chapman's more general assertions in any great detail. On the question of the growth in the number of managers in LT for example, the report confirmed that there had been such an increase, but said that the contention that there were too many managers could not be established 'without a detailed study of all significant parts of LTE'. On the issue of cost-cutting by switching from direct labour to contractors, the report said that further study was needed, and that LT already accepted that there was scope for savings in this and other areas. On management perks (cars, chauffeurs, catering and offices) – for which Chapman had been able to give detailed figures – the report said that a comparison had been made with nationalised industries and private companies; except for the number of chauffeurs, the level of these benefits in LT was found to be similar to that in nationalised industries, and if this comparison was relevant, the level of expenditure was not considered to warrant Chapman's description of it as 'disgraceful'. On the organisation of the cost-cutting unit (the CPU) in London Transport, the report did not pronounce for or against Leslie Chapman's view that the unit would need more external stimulus than LT itself was likely to provide; but plans to move the two top men in the unit back to departmental jobs were criticised. On Chapman's remarks about the mediocrity and complacency of most LT managers, the report said that while there had been some evidence of slowness to act, this was not enough in itself to support the generalised criticisms.

Simultaneously with the submission of the auditors' largely inconclusive report at the end of January, London Transport issued a press release in the name of its chairman, Ralph Bennett, giving its own responses to the Chapman allegations. This statement presented a much less damaging picture of LT's affairs, but Chapman condemned it as an exercise in cosmetics, saying that a careful study of the document revealed it as a mixture of inaccuracies and possibly misleading statements.

In any case, the Deloitte report resulted in no let-up in the bombardment of the LT management. Next to take up the cudgels again was Cutler, who weighed in with a letter of 15 February 1980 to Bennett, expressing bitter disappointment at the responses to some of the Council's directions of the previous December on service levels.

'On the timetabling of buses', the letter went on, 'it seems that once again you cannot deliver the goods either in time or anywhere near what the Council wants . . . On the trains, it seems that your brave promises and bold words [*on agreements with the railway unions, including agreement on extended one-man operation of trains*] have dissolved into prevarication and delays which have become all too familiar.'

For LT the trauma continued when PA International – which, it will be recalled, had been commissioned by the board to carry out a study of the executive management – submitted a largely critical report in April 1980. The consultants' analysis listed a series of alleged failings, of greater or lesser degree, on the part of the LT board – a limited sense of purpose; some smugness; a lack of clarity and agreement on the status and objectives of the undertaking; the lack of a corporate approach in handling problems; a preoccupation with day-to-day problems at the expense of strategic policy issues; inadequate follow-up action after (admittedly good) initial diagnosis; and emphasis on cost rather than value for money. The consultants also came to the conclusion that the board was weak in the skills needed to run a big business, and questioned the usefulness of part-time board members.

In theory the LT board was not obliged to publish the PA International report, since the study had been commissioned by LT itself as an internal exercise. However, Horace Cutler had received a confidential copy and pressed for the report to be made public. Neither he, nor Chapman – nor indeed the firm that had produced the report – was satisfied with London Transport's summarised version, which the board sent to the GLC in May 1980. Cutler said that it soft-pedalled the accusations of inefficiency, while PA International drew attention to what it described as 'important differences in emphasis, strength and in some cases substance between the (LT) memorandum and the PA Report'. Cutler attended a meeting of the board at which the report was discussed and finally forced Ralph Bennett's hand by writing him a letter on 13 June referring to press speculation and calling on him 'now to publish the report, warts and all, both to clear the air and to provide a starting point for the reconstruction work which so patently needs to be done'. When, three days later, Cutler released this letter to the press (as he had said that he would), Bennett gave in and handed out the full PA report for publication.

Predictably, it provided a field-day for the media. Typical was the reaction of the London *Evening News*, which splashed the simple headline 'Guilty', across its front page. Inside, the editorial began with the biting sentence: 'Never has the management of a public service been so coldly exposed and condemned as the Board of London Transport is to-day'. Equally scathing comment came from much of the national press, and from radio and television. But not all the blame was attached to the LT management alone; some side-swipes began to be taken against Cutler and his colleagues. In an article in the London *Evening Standard* a week after the publication of the PA report, the transport journalist Richard Hope commented: 'The impression is that LT is managed to some extent by bumbling idiots. It comes as a shock to recall that most of the idiots were actually appointed by Sir Horace.'

The fear that they might be tarred with the same brush as the LT management did not, however, deter the GLC Conservative leaders from keeping up their sniping attacks on the demoralised Bennett and his colleagues. When, for example, an opposition member suggested at a Council LT Committee meeting at the end of June that a paper on bus maintenance submitted by London Transport included a strong argument for the use of direct labour, the committee chairman (Harold Mote) retorted that 80% of the works throughput referred to in the document had been artificially selected to prove the LT management's own views.

Through most of July, London Transport waited to see what action Cutler would take on the PA International findings. Although Chapman was now sensing a more positive attitude within the LT board, Cutler was clearly under political pressure to make some dramatic changes. On 24 July, on the eve of a special GLC meeting to discuss London Transport's worsening financial plight, Cutler saw Ralph Bennett at County Hall and told him that his appointment as LT chairman was finished; he was to give up his duties at once and go on three months' paid leave. Compensation would be paid for the uncompleted period of his contract, amounting to 2½ years.

On the following day, Bennett's departure was announced, together with details of a big shake-up in the rest of the LT board. One casualty was the uninspired

Stansby, whose appointment as Deputy Chairman was not to be renewed when it ran out two months later; although the chairmanship was to remain vacant for the time being, it was made clear to Stansby that he was not to assume the title of Acting Chairman during the rest of his stay. John Stansby had to some extent fallen from grace since his original appointment in 1978; he had joined in some of his colleagues' strictures on Leslie Chapman's reports, and was thought by Cutler to have succumbed too easily to the 'fleshpots' and 'high living' of the seventh floor at 55 Broadway. He was nevertheless offered further employment in London Transport, though with a lower status, to devote himself to marketing in a board which did without a Deputy Chairman. Understandably he declined this offer, and disappeared back into the world of business consultancy from which he had originally emerged.

Other victims of the shake-up were the Managing Director of the LT Rail System, Bill Maxwell (replaced by the ex-director of the new Hong Kong Metro, Dr Tony Ridley) and the financial member, Jim Glendinning, whose appointment was not to be renewed when it expired at the end of 1980. Dr David Quarmby, the youngest member of the board, was reappointed Managing Director (Buses) for another five years.

The official Council minute about the shake-up also recorded that Leslie Chapman was to have his part-time membership of the board extended for two years from January 1981, but this formal decision was to count for little a few months later when Chapman's continued activity began to turn him into a political embarrassment to the GLC leadership.

There were no courtesies in Cutler's sacking of Ralph Bennett; it was made clear that it was instant dismissal. Immediately after the Council's announcement, Bennett circulated his farewell notice to the LT staff, saying that he would be leaving shortly. A few days later he received a letter from the Council which read:

'My attention has been drawn to a statement which you issued within London Transport on 25 July . . . You will, I am sure understand that I have to-day authorised Mr John Stansby, the Deputy Chairman of London Transport, to make it clearly understood that your responsibilities as Chairman have been relinquished and that accordingly you no longer act as such'.

As a postscript, it should be mentioned that Bennett later won a substantial sum of compensation for the curtailment of his contract.

Bennett's dismissal had been so precipitate that nothing had been done about lining up a successor for the LT chairmanship. When asked on television who would be taking over, Cutler admitted that he had nobody in mind. He has since said that his first choice would have been Sir Freddie Laker, but that Laker had already turned down an earlier offer of a seat on the LT board; given the later collapse of the Laker empire, it may have been just as well for London that he did. It seems that Cutler would have liked a tough, youngish man from the private sector as the new chairman, but such men were not tumbling over themselves to take on a job which three out of the previous four incumbents had had to quit before their time was up, and which offered doubtful rewards for years of exposure to political pressures and, as often as not, public abuse. As the task of finding a new permanent boss for London Transport looked likely to take some time, Cutler decided to appoint a caretaker chairman in the person of Sir Peter Masefield, who, as mentioned earlier, was a part-time board member and came from the world of aviation. Sir Peter, a workaholic who was already 66 at the time of the appointment, was not intended to

Above:
The Jubilee Line opening in 1979. With the Prince of Wales are LT Board members Bennett, Stansby, Maxwell, Quarmby and Glendinning. By early 1981, out of these, only Quarmby was still on the Board. *London Transport*

Left:
Sir Peter Masefield, Chairman of LT 1980-82. *London Transport*

Above:
The London Connection. Sir Peter Masefield (LT) and Sir Peter Parker (BR) at the new Kings Cross (widened lines) station and interchange, 1981. *Ian Allan Library*

Below:
The Hammersmith station site. This shows a model of one of the successive LT development schemes blocked by planners and politicians.
London Transport

stay in the post for more than a 12-month period at the outside; in the event he was to remain as Chairman and Chief Executive for over two years while successive GLC leaderships, Tory and Socialist, struggled with the problem of finding someone of sufficient calibre who was willing to take the job on as a permanency.

Having given the LT board a new look and installed Masefield as its stop-gap boss, the administration at County Hall was now hoping that all the public outcry about the management of London Transport would be allowed to die down in a run-up to the 1981 GLC election. But in this hope it was to be disappointed.

Masefield offered Chapman the opportunity of chairing a Productivity Committee at board level, but Chapman thought that the committee would be remote from the mainstream of LT management and would in any case lack teeth; in a characteristic reply to Masefield's offer, he turned the post down as a 'non-job'. Rather oddly, Chapman had not agreed with the precipitate sacking of Bennett and the revamping of the board, even though they were to no small extent due to his own activities. He apparently felt that the old board had learnt its lesson and should have been allowed to work its passage back to respectability, with gradual rather than sudden changes. So it was perhaps not surprising that he soon found himself in a minority on the new board, just as he had originally been on the old one. In particular he fell foul of Peter Masefield, who was later to describe Chapman as 'not my favourite person'.

Masefield's main row with Chapman was over the confidentiality of the board's internal discussions and affairs. It was not merely a question of Chapman's taking his differences with his colleagues to the GLC; this he considered his right, and in some cases his duty. But he also responded freely to the approaches of the media, who saw in him a continuing source of eye and ear-catching copy. Matters came to the crunch at the formal monthly meeting of the LT board in November 1980, when the recording of a broadcast by Chapman was played over to the assembled members; an unpleasant scene followed, at the end of which Chapman left – or was asked to leave – the meeting. His reaction was to go to Cutler and ask if he could quit London Transport at the end of 1980 in accordance with the terms of his original appointment, so giving up the two years' extension of his term of office for which the Council had voted in July.

Cutler was in a political dilemma of his own making. If he agreed to Chapman's request to stand down, there would be a lot of difficult explaining to be done and a lot of press coverage on the theme of 'the Axeman Axed'. If he persuaded Chapman to stay on in LT, there could be a rebellion in the LT boardroom which would rock the board in the critical period leading up to the Spring 1981 Council election. Cutler's immediate response was to ask Chapman to remain and try, with Council backing, to ride out his dispute with Masefield and the board. Cutler followed this request with a letter on 13 November to confirm that he did not propose to ask the Council to revise or rescind its decision on 25 July on Chapman's reappointment.

However, when Masefield and several of his board colleagues made it clear that they would resign if Chapman stayed, Cutler was forced to go back on the Council decision and turn Chapman away. Politically he could not face a series of resignations from the LT board at such a critical time, and so soon after he had reorganised it. To Chapman, Cutler blamed his volte-face on an agreement which he had reached with Andrew McIntosh, the moderate leader of the Labour opposition, not to limit the next GLC administration's freedom of action by making any further appointments to the London Transport board extending beyond April 1981. According to Chapman, McIntosh later told him that he had no recollection of any such agreement.

Of course, the dropping of Chapman from the LT scene did not go unremarked by the media, and Horace Cutler was given a rough ride on the subject in a *World in Action* television programme in April 1981. Altogether Cutler's gamble in bringing the axeman into London Transport had not paid off. How badly the idea had backfired is shown by the fact that Chapman was reported to have advised people to vote Labour in the run-up to the GLC election.

Looking back on how Chapman came to be appointed to the LT board in 1978, it is possible to see why his assignment achieved only limited success. Cutler's decision to make the appointment seems to have been due, at least in part, to the desire to add to the range of Council pressures on London Transport. On the other hand, Chapman, still sore from his unhappy experiences with the civil service, was out to expose waste wherever he could find it, and was not prepared to be muzzled either by his board colleagues or by the politicians who had appointed him. Of course there was – and still is – scope for better management and significant cost savings in London Transport (as indeed the economy and productivity drive by the present LT Chairman has shown). But Chapman's aims were not best served by the high profile which he adopted and the atmosphere of scandal which he generated in his dealings with LT. In the event, his intervention seems to have achieved little of value. Admittedly the productivity organisation which was set up during his appointment still functions. But it should be remembered that a number of moves to economise in costs and manpower had already been initiated before Leslie Chapman ever appeared on the scene; examples were the switch to one-man bus operation over large parts of London, the extension of automatic 'programmed' signalling, and the progressive modernisation and automation of the power supply system on the Underground. And undoubtedly more such moves would have bean made, as a result of internal initiatives as well as external pressures, even if Chapman had never joined London Transport. How far Chapman stimulated the process during his turbulent stay with LT is a moot point.

Despite later assertions to the contrary, Chapman's public criticisms of London Transport – whether warranted or not – did hit the morale of the staff, and not only at top management level. Many who had worked hard all their lives, often in difficult conditions and with irregular working hours, under the impression that they were helping to provide a valuable service to the community, suddenly felt that they were being branded as wasters and parasites. The notable boost that Sir Peter Masefield gave to London Transport during his extended caretaker chairmanship in the post-Chapman period was due less to his executive skill – in fact he found it hard to delegate – than to his ability to restore some of the undertaking's tarnished reputation and give the staff back some of their lost self-respect.

It is interesting to speculate whether, if Chapman had not been appointed to London Transport, Ralph Bennett might have survived as chairman. Admittedly Cutler was already disillusioned with Bennett before Chapman joined LT and the PA International report might by itself have provided enough grounds for Bennett's dismissal. But it is conceivable that without Chapman's accusations, Bennett might have managed to last until the Spring 1981 GLC elections and then won a reprieve from the new Labour administration at County Hall.

6
Ken Livingstone and the Fares Fiasco

So far in the 1980s, the London Transport scene has been dominated for much of the time by the politically emotive question of fares and subsidies, and the undertaking has suffered the worst see-sawing of fare levels in its history.

During 1980 LT fares were twice increased – by nearly 20% in February/March and by over 13% in September. These heavy rises were brought in to cover unexpectedly large increases in costs, including pay increases averaging 20% which, for the first time in five years, had had to be negotiated without the constraints imposed by a Government incomes policy. So, despite the fact that more staff and vehicles were available in 1980 and there was an improvement in the services, the passenger-mileage dropped by 4% compared with the previous year. Although this drop could be primarily attributed to the increased fares, part of it was clearly due to the growing economic recession.

In May 1981 Labour won the GLC election with a narrow majority of votes (42%

Below:
Real LT fare levels 1972-1984 – quarterly indices. *R. Armstrong*

Labour, 40% Conservative) but with a working majority of seats (50 out of 92), so ousting Horace Cutler and his administration. The much divided Labour group had fought the election under the banner of its moderate leader Andrew McIntosh, a dedicated and intelligent man who had been much involved in London Transport's affairs while in opposition. Sadly he was not to taste the fruits of victory and become Leader of the Council. Immediately after the election, he was voted out of the leadership by the now dominant left-wing bloc in the Labour group, and the egregious and controversial Ken Livingstone was awarded the prize. At the same time, the left wing presented a complete list of chairmen and vice-chairmen for all the committees in the new Labour council, and voted them into office en bloc. Among them was Dave Wetzel, a one-time London bus inspector, who was given the chairmanship of the Transport Committee. As a footnote to the story of this left-wing coup at County Hall, it should be mentioned that when, at a later date, Michael Foot was seeking to strengthen the Labour Party's representation in the House of Lords, Andrew McIntosh became – albeit rather reluctantly – a life peer.

In its election manifesto, the GLC Labour group had promised a 25% cut in London Transport fares and other travel concessions (the so-called 'Fares Fair' programme) if it won. So, soon after taking office, the new Labour Council called on LT to put forward proposals for the cut as quickly as possible. The first evidence of the new Council's transport policies was the extension of free travel for the elderly to the Underground system; this took place in June 1981. The main change came on 4 October 1981, when fares were reduced by an average of 32% – even more than Labour had promised – and a major step was taken towards further simplifying the fares system by extending zone fares to the whole of the bus network and introducing them on the Underground in Central London.

The massive reduction in fares brought the average price of travel on London Transport down to the level at which, in real terms, it had stood in 1969. The result was an increase from 5½ million to six million in the number of daily passengers using LT buses and trains, and a small but worthwhile reduction in the use of cars in Central London and in the level of traffic congestion. On the other hand, the fares cut raised the subsidy to be paid by London's ratepayers by £125million in a full year, and aroused a storm of protest from domestic ratepayers, from firms which were already considering leaving the capital or closing down altogether because of London's high rates and rents, and from many of the London Boroughs. To all these protesters the increased rates demand appeared especially unfair because a very high proportion of those benefiting from the lower fares were not even residents of Greater London, but commuted into the City and West End daily from beyond the GLC area or were simply visitors from the provinces and abroad. The ratepayers felt that they were being asked to pay through the nose to benefit others who were not making the same sacrifice. Their wrath was understandable, although a large part of the total subsidy to LT after October 1981 was still being provided by Central Government, and the rise in the total amount of subsidy to LT (from 29% of total costs to 56%) had only brought London's public transport subsidy level into line with that of such cities as Paris and Chicago.

One of the London Boroughs – Bromley – decided to contest the 'Fares Fair' policy of Ken Livingstone's administration at County Hall, and challenged the GLC's legal right under the Transport (London) Act of 1969 to order the big cut in fares. At the initial hearing in the Divisional Court, the judgment went in favour of the GLC, but Bromley then took the case to the Court of Appeal under Lord Denning, where that judgment was reversed. The GLC then decided to carry the case on to the House of Lords, where five Law Lords ruled on 17 December 1981 that the findings of the

Left:
Ken Livingstone, the GLC Leader, leaves the Law Courts after three judges rule the 1983 fares reduction legal. *Press Association*

Below:
Dave Wetzel, GLC Transport Committee Chairman, tries out an experimental ticket machine. *Ian Allan Library*

Above:
An unimpressed audience. Dave Wetzel speaks at the Westbourne Park bus garage opening, 1981. *LT News*

Below:
Blake Hall station. Obliged to keep the rural Epping-Ongar line open with inadequate financing, LT closed this almost unused station in 1981 to help cut costs. *Ian Allan Library*

Appeal Court should stand and that the reduced fares were unlawful under the 1969 Act. According to the Law Lords' interpretation of the Act, London Transport had to plan, as far as it could, to operate on a commercial basis and break even in each accounting period; any unavoidable shortfall in one year must be made good in the next. The Lords' judgment also indicated that in introducing any fares cut, the GLC had to take account of its duty as trustee for the ratepayers of London as well as the interests of the travelling public.

As may be imagined, the Law Lords' judgment caused consternation at County Hall. Livingstone and Wetzel complained sharply that the judgment was a political one, made undemocratically by non-elected judges against a policy which had figured in the manifesto on which Labour had won the GLC election. In fact, of course, the Transport (London) Act of 1969 was the law of the land, democratically enacted by Parliament, and the Law Lords' findings were no more than their legal interpretation of the somewhat imprecise rights and duties laid on London Transport and the GLC by that Act.

There were conflicting legal opinions on what action the GLC now needed to take to bring itself within the law, since the Law Lords' judgment had still not made it clear to what extent – if any – tax and rates subsidies for London Transport could be considered legal. By early 1982 the Council had accepted reluctantly that it would have to change its policy towards LT radically to comply with the law. London Transport was ordered to produce a revised budget for 1982 incorporating a huge and early fares increase, a reduction in services to achieve major cost savings, and a severe and on-going economy drive. A revised budget on these lines was quickly endorsed by a chastened but still resentful GLC and at the earliest possible date – 21 March 1982 – a fares increase averaging a colossal 96% was introduced on London's buses and Underground trains. This meant that within the last quarter of 1981 and the first quarter of 1982, London Transport had had to suffer the absurdity of having its fares first cut by nearly a third and then virtually doubled. The net effect of these violent swings was that fares at the end of March 1982 were a third higher on average than they had been at the beginning of October 1981.

In doubling its fares early in 1982 to comply with the Lords' judgment, London Transport maintained the simplified fares structure that it had adopted for the Fares Fair changes. LT traffic, so recently stimulated by Fares Fair, fell again from six to five million passengers per day after the fares were doubled, and there was a corresponding worsening in street congestion; but the London ratepayers' contribution to LT's finances was reduced by over £200million in a full year, and the percentage of total LT expenditure covered by subsidies was cut to only 27% – almost the lowest degree of subsidisation of any major city transport system in the world.

If the Fares Fair cut was excessive – and under British conditions it probably was – the subsequent doubling of fares under the Law Lords' ruling clearly went too far in the opposite direction. London Transport carried out a cost-benefit analysis which showed that, at the level of subsidy in the latter part of 1982, every extra £1 of subsidy would produce benefits to the community worth £1.40 in terms of lower fares, improved services, and reductions in road traffic congestion, road accidents, noise and pollution. Even Conservatives in the GLC and elsewhere acknowledged that after the March 1982 fares increase the price of travel on London Transport was too high and the level of subsidy too low. In June 1982, the Conservative *Daily Telegraph* went so far as to publish an article in which, to quote the blurb, Professor Ezra Mishan 'swept away many of the fallacies that had confused the debate about the proper level of fares on London's transport system'. Interestingly, in addition to demonstrating the net public benefit of increasing support to public transport and penalising the private car in cities, Professor Mishan suggested that because of London Transport's vital importance to the functioning of London as the nation's administrative and commercial capital, most if not all of the subsidy to the undertaking should come from general taxation rather than from the London ratepayer.

By mid-1982 David Howell, Secretary of State for Transport in the Conservative Government which had ousted the Callaghan administration in 1979, had accepted that the level of London fares following the Law Lords' ruling was too high, and was seeking ways of establishing a more stable and legally secure basis for reasonable levels of subsidy to urban public transport. The Government even asked the GLC to consult the public over ways in which London fares might be reduced in the following year, and the Council accordingly commissioned an opinion poll and inserted notices in the press to obtain Londoners' views on five different fares and service options, varying from the Break Even approach at one extreme to the Fares Fair approach at the other.

The GLC's external researches and wordy internal debates during the rest of 1982 culminated in a so-called Balanced Plan which the Council believed would satisfy the requirements of the 1969 Act and strike an acceptable balance between the interests of the ratepayers and passengers in the Greater London Area. In this plan, the fares system would be further simplified and there would be an average reduction of 25% from the post-Law Lords fares levels.

On 15 December 1982 the GLC issued a formal direction to London Transport, requiring it to implement this 25% cut in the following Spring. But LT was told by its legal advisers that in their opinion the cut would be illegal under the 1969 Act, just as the earlier Fares Fair cut had proved to be. So, mindful of the damaging upheaval that it had suffered as a result of Fares Fair, LT contested the Council's power to issue the directive. The GLC's response was to take its Balanced Plan to the High Court for a ruling on its legality.

At the end of January 1983 the High Court ruled that the new plan, with its 25% average cut in fares and £100million increase in the subsidy to LT, was a proper and legal exercise of the GLC's powers under the 1969 Act. In delivering the Court's verdict, Lord Justice Kerr said that the plan was totally different from the Fares Fair scheme against which the House of Lords had pronounced just over a year earlier. The new plan had been carefully formulated on legal advice and after full consultation, and was based on a 'carefully researched strategy for transport in London as a whole'. It did not derive from an election manifesto, nor was it the preferred option of the Labour majority in the GLC. It represented, said the judge, a 'reluctant compromise' between the heavily-subsidised Fares Fair scheme on the one hand and a situation in which LT would break even financially on the other hand; and it did not impose an unfair burden on ratepayers.

One of the other two judges, Mr Justice Glidewell, said that the earlier Fares Fair scheme had made no attempt to strike a balance between the duties owed to passengers and ratepayers. It did not follow from that, however, that the GLC had no power to subsidise fares; it had to exercise that power within limits, and the new Balanced Plan fell within those limits. The remaining judge, Mr Justice Nolan, said that if it were not practicable for London Transport to break even, it could lawfully operate at a deficit, and the GLC could lawfully finance that deficit by subsidy.

One odd result of the High Court judgment was that London Transport had to pay court costs of £14,000. This was because LT lawyers had opposed the GLC order on the Balanced Plan as being illegal. But a London Transport spokesman emphasised that the case had been a 'friendly action' and added 'Our concern was that we should keep within the law. We ourselves felt that fares were too high, and said so in court'.

The reaction of the GLC's Labour leaders was one of muted triumph. As the High Court judges retired after giving their judgment, Dave Wetzel sped them on their way with a shouted 'Thank you very much'. Ken Livingstone, who had previously accused the judges of showing political bias in their findings, commented smugly: 'We never said that every judge was nasty'.

On the Conservative side, Alan Greengross, then deputy leader (now Leader) of the Opposition in the GLC, said that he and his colleagues had already accepted that fares needed cutting; but he felt that they could be kept down by improving the efficiency and productivity of London Transport rather than by simply increasing the rates.

Soon after the High Court action, there was a further development which cast fresh doubt on the acceptability of the proposed 25% fares cut. This was the passage of the Transport Act 1983 which – among other things – authorised the Transport Secretary to lay down guidelines for public transport subsidies in Greater London and each of the metropolitan counties. Subsidies within the guidelines were protected against legal challenge by ratepayers or local boroughs; subsidies beyond the guidelines were not so protected and could also incur Government penalties. In the case of Greater London, the Council's proposed figure of support to LT for the financial year 1983/84 (£235million, including provision for the fares cut) was greatly in excess of the Transport Secretary's guideline (£125million). So, before voting the money for its Balanced Plan, the GLC again sought the opinion of its legal adviser, Roger Henderson, QC. His advice was that the £235million grant would be lawful if certain conditions were met. The first was that the GLC's decision on the level of grant should be 'reached with an open mind, taking the Secretary of State's guidance into account'. The second was that Council members should consider such a grant necessary to fulfil their statutory duty to provide adequate public transport services in London. The third was that 'a fair balance between all ratepayers and other interested parties – particularly public transport passengers – was being kept'.

Reassured by this advice, a meeting of the full Greater London Council early in May 1983 voted the money for the Balanced Plan, and on 22 May the 25% cut in fares was duty made. This reduction was accompanied by a further big simplification of the fare structure. On the bus system, the two central fare zones were combined, so that the whole system is now covered by only three concentric fare zones – central, inner and outer. On the Underground, the two central fare zones were similarly combined into a single zone (Zone 1), and the rest of the network was divided into four concentric zones (Zones 2, 3a, 3b and 3c). But perhaps the greatest innovation was the introduction of the Travelcard, replacing almost all Underground season tickets and many bus passes. Passengers can now buy Travelcards for the zones in which they travel regularly, and these cards can be used as required in those particular zones, not only of the Underground but also – at no extra cost – on the buses.

The fares cut of May 1983 brought the average level of London Transport fares back almost exactly to what it had been when Ken Livingstone and his colleagues took over at County Hall two years earlier. It is tempting to think that if Livingstone had simply announced a fares freeze when he first came to office, this would probably have gone unchallenged and the public would have enjoyed the benefits of a substantial saving in the real price of travel in London (due to subsequent

Above:
London bus fare zones since 1983. *R. Armstrong*

inflation in general prices) without all the legal wrangles and the upheavals to London Transport and its passengers caused by the ridiculous down-up-down fares 'yo-yo' of the past few years.

It is clear that this experience was one of the main reasons why the Thatcher Government decided to take the political responsibility for public transport in London out of the hands of the Greater London Council and transfer it back to Central Government. As the then Transport Secretary, David Howell, said in the run-up to the June 1983 General Election: 'We are determined that London Transport shall cease to be the political football it has become under the GLC.' The recent history of London fares may, indeed, also turn out to have been one of the larger nails in the GLC's own coffin.

Perhaps the only benefit of the violent changes in the LT fares since 1981 is that they provided the opportunity to simplify the fares structure to a degree and at a pace which might not otherwise have been possible. Certainly, in the course of its 50 years as a single undertaking, London Transport has never had such a simple basic fares system as it has to-day, and it is hoping to carry the process of simplifying and integrating its fares still further in the future.

Allowing for cost escalation in the two intervening years, the 1983 level of LT fares involved a higher degree of subsidy than before the 1981 Fares Fair scheme. By contrast, there is evidence that over the same period, other countries were trying to reduce their high level of subsidy to city transport undertakings. To quote from the foreword of a recent reference book on urban transport systems: 'All over the world

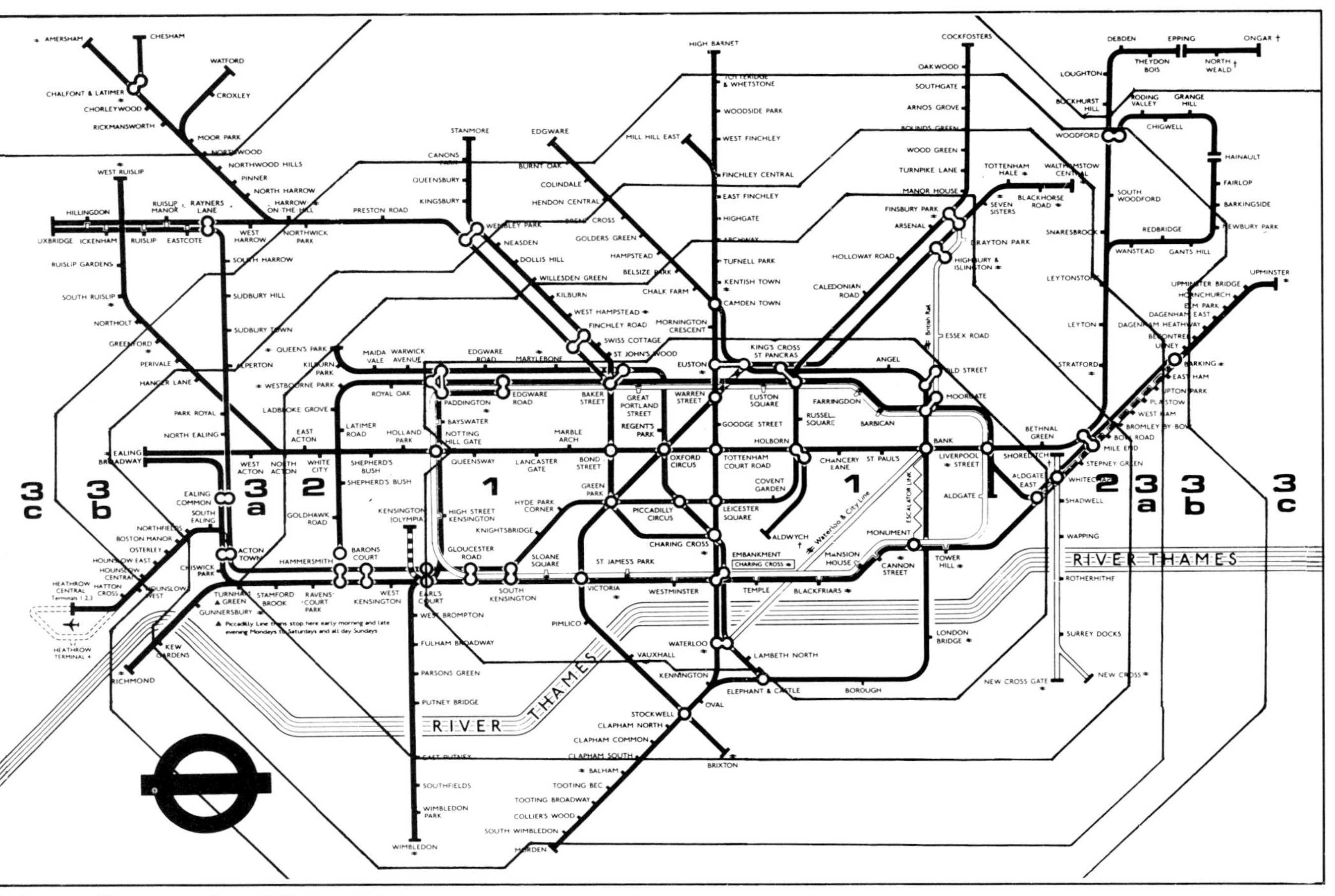

Underground fare zones since 1983. *Copyright London Regional Transport*

there is pressure, generally from central government, for public transport to make do with less external support.' The foreword goes on to suggest that urban public transport systems, grappling with the problem of reduced passenger revenue in a recession, have been dealt a severe blow by cuts in financial support imposed by politicians for budgeting reasons quite unconnected with the merits of public transport or the long-term need for support, investment and renewal. But even with this widespread trend towards reduced subsidisation of public transport abroad, London Transport still remains towards the lower end of the world subsidy 'league'.

There have been one or two other interesting developments in the field of LT fares and subsidisation in the last few years. Towards the end of 1982, for example, the GLC agreed to increase the payments made to London Transport for free bus and Underground travel for the capital's elderly. The increase, amounting to some £3million on a payment of about £50million a year, still fell short of what LT considered necessary to meet the proper cost of this social service, including the cost of carrying the so-called 'generated' traffic, ie, old people who, but for the free facility, would not have travelled at all. And even this limited improvement in the basis of the GLC's payments for old people's free travel represented only a victory of principle for London Transport, since the Council decided at the same time that the additional payment for old people should be offset by a corresponding reduction in its general revenue subsidy to LT.

Another development in the 1980s concerned the contributions made by the counties around Greater London to the net losses incurred by London Transport in operating bus and Underground services beyond the Greater London boundaries. On bus services of this kind, much – but not all – of the loss was met by the counties, and London Transport reduced the shortfall by trimming the services and charging special premium fares on them. The net loss on Underground lines extending outside the GLC area was considerably greater, and despite similar sanctions by London Transport to those applied on the out-county bus services, the counties' contribution to LT lines in their areas was relatively small (for example, some £1½million towards an estimated £9million loss in the 1982/83 financial year). In particular, Essex County Council stopped making any contribution towards the losses incurred on the Underground lines in Essex, with the result that London Transport withdrew all except the weekday peak-hour services on the Epping-Ongar line, as well as the evening service on the Woodford-Hainault line. A fresh application by London Transport in 1980 to close the Epping-Ongar line altogether had been met in March 1981 by another refusal from the Transport Secretary, although his decision was stated to apply 'for the time being'.

7 Under New Management

In addition to the successive swings in London Transport's fares and subsidy levels so far in the 1980s, there have also been big changes in its organisation and top personalities. In September 1980 – soon after the dismissal of Ralph Bennett as LT Chairman and his replacement on a caretaker basis by Sir Peter Masefield – the last stages of the reorganisation planned under the already departed John Stansby came into effect. It involved the creation of a new Main Board with a co-ordinating role, and three subsidiary boards controlling London Transport's principal businesses – a Rail Board, a Bus Board and a Property Board. Although each of these businesses had its own Managing Director, Masefield acted as Chairman not only of the Main Board but also of the Rail and Bus Boards as well. Under these two operational boards, a direct line of management led down to four Railway Divisions and eight Bus Districts, each with its own General Manager. The stated purpose of the changes was to clarify lines of management and financial control, and delegate more decision-making to local managements with a fuller knowledge of conditions in their areas.

Mention has been made earlier of Sir Peter Masefield's management style. Unlike one of his predecessors (Sir Kenneth Robinson, who ordered committees to be pruned and meetings curtailed wherever possible in London Transport) Masefield was very much a committee man; but his policy of personal involvement in all fields of LT activity was clearly designed to restore confidence and build up morale among managers and staff after the unhappy experiences of the Cutler-Chapman era. In this purpose he was largely successful. In the foreword to London Transport's Annual Report for 1982, the present Chairman, Dr Keith Bright, thanked the staff for their efforts during a difficult year and added: 'In particular, I would like to pay tribute to my predecessor, Sir Peter Masefield, whose steadying hand and influence made such a contribution to London Transport at a time when it was perhaps needed as much as at any other time in its history.'

Masefield's appointment as a stop-gap Chairman and Chief Executive in August 1980 had been intended to run for a mere 6-12 months while a full-term successor was being recruited. But because of the delay in finding a volunteer of the right pedigree to take on a job involving 'more kicks than ha'pence', Masefield was twice asked to extend his appointment, and did not finally step down until the end of August 1982. The GLC had taken the altogether unprecedented step of advertising the Chairmanship of London Transport in the Press, and – with the left-wing Labour faction under Ken Livingstone in control at County Hall after May 1981 – there were fears that some off-beat or extremist candidate might be put into this key post. In the event, however, wiser counsels prevailed, the candidate appointed to the job for a five-year term from September 1982 being a business man from the private sector, in the person of Dr Bright, who had previously managed the Huntley & Palmer food empire.

Since retiring from his London Transport post, Sir Peter Masefield has made one useful contribution to the debate on the future of public transport in this country. In a valuable review of the British transport scene, presented to a meeting of the Chartered Institute of Transport in London in December 1982, Masefield welcomed the Government's White Paper on 'Public Transport Subsidy in Cities' of the previous month (foreshadowing the Transport Act of 1983), which acknowledged that efficient transport was vital to the life of our great cities and said that a clear and consistent legal framework was needed for the payment of reasonable amounts of subsidy. Building on this acceptance by the Government that a sensible level of subsidy for urban public transport was lawful, Masefield argued for an overall subsidy (revenue plus capital), from taxes and rates together, amounting to a fixed 50% of costs, based on agreed maximum fares and levels of service. Although it would still fall short of subsidy levels abroad, such an arrangement would, he contended, be easily understood, eliminate politically inspired ups and downs, give much needed stability to the industry, and encourage good but cost-effective standards of service. Whether or not the figure of 50% is a sound and acceptable one, the idea of a political consensus on a fixed percentage of subsidy for urban public transport – subject to cost, fare and service safeguards – is an interesting one.

Dr Bright's management style and policy objectives since his appointment to the top LT job have differed widely from those of Sir Peter Masefield. The whole drive of Bright's policy has been to cut costs and increase efficiency and productivity wherever possible in the undertaking without worsening the service to the public. To pursue this course more effectively, he tended initially to take up a rather detached position and avoid too much personal involvement. One of his early changes was to set up a new Executive Committee, consisting of the Board Members and three of the functional directors, to 'oversee the routine management of the organisation, the management of change and the development of policies'. This single body replaced a number of different committees which had flourished under the Masefield regime.

Within the first six or seven months of Dr Bright's arrival at 55 Broadway, a variety of developments and proposals were announced, which – while they might not be wholly or even partly attributable to the new Chairman's initiatives – were certainly very much in line with his thinking. Thus, for example, a report was submitted to the GLC late in 1982, based on the results of an expert inquiry, proposing that in order to achieve further savings in the cost of supplying electricity to the Underground, London Transport should phase out its own power stations in the next 10 to 15 years and take all its requirements from the national grid. Strangely enough, this proposal was questioned by the GLC Transport Committee on the very grounds on which LT itself had based its previous policy of generating its own electricity – the reliability of power supplies to the deep-level tube lines in emergency.

Another cost-cutting proposal, mooted early in 1983, involved the reduction of the number of bus management districts from eight to six. Considerable savings in administrative costs were expected from this change (since carried out), but it did represent something of a volte-face, since the local management framework for LT bus operations had been expanded from four geographical divisions to eight districts under the Stansby reorganisation little more than three years earlier.

Yet another attack on London Transport's costs was launched in March 1983, when the Secretary of State for Trade announced that the Monopolies Commission had been asked to investigate the efficiency of the undertaking's bus maintenance activities. David Howell, who was Transport Secretary when the announcement was made, justified the reference to the Commission in these words:

'LT's bus maintenance is big business. It costs about £80million a year to maintain London Transport's fleet of more than 5,000 buses. Since more than half of the total cost of LT's bus operation is covered by subsidy from taxpayers and ratepayers, the public is entitled to know if it is getting best value for money.'

London Transport itself offered full co-operation in the inquiry, saying that while it had a first-class bus safety record and was already making real progress towards improving its engineering efficiency, it would welcome any helpful ideas for further savings which the Commission might produce.

Besides adding new impetus to the search for major economies in London Transport, Dr Bright also put his weight behind a long-needed blitz on fare dodging. Towards the end of 1982 a special new Underground 'task force' was set up to intensify spot checks for fare bilkers at selected stations, and by March 1983 over 350 people had been convicted and hundreds more were waiting to appear in court. During one month, six special court sessions had to be held, each hearing between 30 and 40 cases, and the penalties and costs in individual cases were as high as £100. In June 1983 more plans to crack down on fare evasion were outlined in a report to the Greater London Council, including more ticket inspection on both the bus and rail networks, swoops by bus inspectors in the worst areas, more Underground booking clerks and ticket machines, and a system of receipts for excess fares. Ticket-dodging and fraud were estimated to be costing London Transport no less than £30million a year in lost revenue, and this loss had to be made up by the vast majority of honest passengers or by the taxpayer and ratepayer. Dr Ridley, Managing Director of the Underground, stressed that fare fiddling was not, as many people seemed to regard it, a socially acceptable practice. 'It is theft, and in the past year more than 5,000 people have acquired criminal records for fares offences and many more cases are in the pipeline.'

One man above all others – Leslie Chapman, the 'axeman' – might have been expected to acclaim Dr Bright's initiatives to cut London Transport's costs and fraud losses, and to find in them a justification for his own earlier strictures on the undertaking. In practice, Chapman chose the very time when Bright's drive was beginning to bite – the spring of 1983 – to launch a new campaign to dispute LT board members' right to select their own official cars and decide on their own perks.

Chapman had by this time set up a charity called Waste in Public Expenditure Ltd to expose cases of extravagance by public authorities, and had succeeded in getting it accepted by the Charity Commissioners. The charity was reported as involving close members of Chapman's family only at that stage, and was not seeking public funds or donations. Instead it was to rely for funds on the income from Chapman's two best-selling books – *Your Disobedient Servant* and *Waste Away* – and his other writings, as well as fees from his television appearances.

The newspapers quickly picked up the story of Leslie Chapman's new attack on the LT board, and highlighted the fact that Dr Bright had the exclusive use of a W registration Aston Martin car acquired from his previous employers, Huntley & Palmer, as well as the occasional use of a chauffeur-driven Ford Granada. Under an eye-catching headline reading 'Charity team looks into £30,000 LT perk', the London *Standard* gave its version of the facts, with a well-timed photograph showing Dr Bright on crutches outside his home, looking back ruefully at the parked Aston Martin before getting into the Granada to be driven to work. The article explained that Bright had recently been using the chauffeur-driven Granada, rather than the Aston Martin, because he had broken his foot and could not drive.

Leslie Chapman was quoted by the *Standard* as saying:

Right:
Dr Keith Bright, Chairman of LT from 1982. *London Transport*

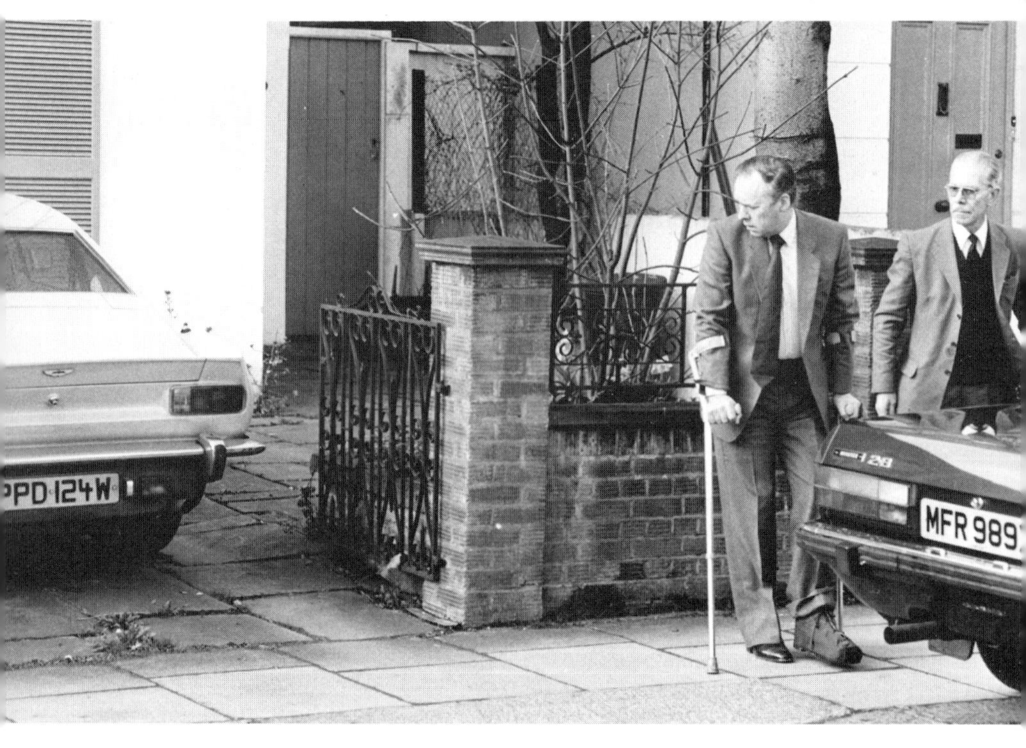

Below:
The 'perks' row, April 1983. Dr Bright glances at the LT-hired Aston Martin before being driven to work. *Express Newspapers*

'I have no views on Dr Bright's cars, but I am not happy with the answers I have so far been given as to the legal question. Any group of people wholly or partly in charge of public funds should not be able to determine what their own various emoluments should be. The 1969 Act intended to ensure that though the Executive Board determine these things for the staff, they could not determine it for themselves. I have taken legal soundings and believe there is something here which needs to be examined more closely. If, on the other hand, the GLC and London Transport are right about this matter, then I think the ratepayers should know about it.'

London Transport's views on this legal issue were also given in the *Standard* article. A spokesman said:

'The Act says nothing about conditions of service, travel benefits and holidays. A car is not a salary, fee or pension and it is not our view that the Act requires GLC approval for such a condition of service. The contract between the GLC and board members also says nothing about these matters. Their conditions of service are based on those of its most senior staff and those of its predecessors and are well known to the GLC.'

On the day after the *Standard* article, the *Daily Telegraph* took up the tale, saying that the Chairman's Aston Martin was among 185 cars hired by London Transport for use by its staff. The paper acknowledged that many of these cars were used by lower-level staff, such as local bus managers, on a shared basis, to 'get around London quicker than they would on the buses they organise', but omitted to mention that they were mostly modest vehicles which were often invaluable in the operational control of the bus system.

LT was quick to point out that the now famous – or infamous – Aston Martin had been bought by Huntley & Palmer from its original private owner. 'So it was second hand to them and is third hand to us', said the spokesman. Although it might have cost £30,000 when new, its value was then more like £15,000; and it had in any case not been bought by London Transport but was merely hired from the Avis car-hire firm. In any case, said the LT statement, 'we believe a car is an essential part of the package offered to get the best possible senior staff for London Transport'.

Whatever he may have felt about Leslie Chapman's public attacks on the relatively minor issue of LT board members' emoluments, Dr Bright kept his eye firmly fixed on the target of major savings in the undertaking. By May 1983 he was able to report that by 'hard' management, savings were being identified at the rate of £100,000 a week. There were, he said, good opportunities for further savings by extending one-man operation of buses and trains, and by cutting large central overhead costs. He added that between £1million and £2million could be saved by 'moving people around and cutting the size of some of the offices'. This process presumably included his own move from the enormous office, occupied for over 50 years by successive LT Chairmen, to more modest accommodation on the same floor in the 55 Broadway headquarters; the vast Chairman's Office, listed for preservation as part of the Holden-designed building, was already doubling as LT's main boardroom, but its more intensive use for other meetings has enabled other conference rooms to be converted to office use.

Cutting costs and increasing productivity means, of course, fewer jobs, and the staff employed by London Transport at the end of 1982 were nearly 1,700 fewer than at the end of 1981. By the end of the first quarter of 1983, manpower had been cut by a further 300. This continuous shedding of LT staff might have been something of an embarrassment to Ken Livingstone and his leftist colleagues in the Greater London Council, since they are dedicated to saving jobs in London but were themselves responsible for Dr Bright's appointment to LT. Perhaps they accepted, after the Law Lords' ruling in December 1981, that cuts in LT staff were inevitable. Anyway, they kept a low profile on the subject for some time, although a protest was voiced by Dave Wetzel, the GLC Transport Committee Chairman, in March 1983, when he argued that any further large-scale extension of one-man operation on London buses would be a false economy. In any case the GLC leadership were to some extent themselves offsetting cuts in LT staff by recruiting more people into the Council's own employ, many of them to staff a variety of dubious and sometimes bizarre fringe activities invented since they came into office in County Hall.

Looking at London Transport as it was when Keith Bright took over the chairmanship in 1982, it is clear that the time was ripe for a new and determined campaign to cut costs and raise efficiency in the undertaking. This was needed not only as a duty to the public, but also to justify the claim that even the most cost-effective public transport system needs to be subsidised on a considerable scale if the community is to get the best and most economical overall transport deal.

London Transport's efficiency levels have often been compared unfavourably with those of other operators elsewhere. In a recent report setting out bus efficiency trends in Britain in the 1970s, the Polytechnic of Central London recorded that in 1979-80, for every 100 bus miles per employee produced by small local bus undertakings around Britain, the provincial city undertakings (PTEs) produced 90, while the London bus system could manage no more than 65. Because of heavier bus loadings in London, the corresponding comparison of passengers per bus employee was less unfavourable to LT, the ratio in that case being 100:95:80. The explanation for the big disparity in the productivity levels is simple; in small towns and the provincial cities, most if not all of the buses can be one-man operated, whereas in London many of the buses have to run for mile after mile through congested city streets, and have to carry a conductor if they are not to suffer intolerable delays at bus stops.

However, Dr Bright made it clear that he did not want this and other special London conditions to be used as an excuse for inaction in seeking economies. In the spring of 1983, when introducing the previous year's annual report, he said: 'There are many good reasons why certain productivity indices are worse in London Transport than elsewhere, but there are no good reasons for not seeking to improve them.' In line with this philosophy, the percentage of LT bus services worked by one-man operated buses was increased from 48% to 53% in April 1983, reducing the number of conductors by 500. The prospects of further extending one-man bus operation in London have been enhanced by the new and simpler fares introduced in May 1983, and in particular by the new Travelcards. But there would still seem to be a limit beyond which, under London conditions, more one-man bus operation would be counter-productive. In the protest which, as mentioned earlier, Dave Wetzel made against converting too much of the LT bus system to one-man operation, he pointed out that although the undertaking would save some £60million a year by dispensing with all its remaining conductors, this sum would be completely offset by the higher wages paid to the driver-operators, the costs of slower bus running and the costs of poorer bus regularity; in addition, there would be the capital cost of replacing over 2,000 crew-operated Routemaster buses, plus – from the community standpoint – a reduction in passenger convenience because of the poorer service (valued at roundly £40million a year) and the cost of keeping some, at least, of the displaced conductors on the dole.

There are other areas, too, in which cuts may prove counter-productive if carried too far or made too fast. Unless care is taken, it is all too easy to throw the baby out with the bathwater. One field in which significant cuts have been made during the course of the present LT economy drive is that of senior and middle management. In the past year or two, many managers and senior officials have left the service of London Transport by taking early retirement on agreed terms, without replacement. There is undoubtedly a case for many of these cuts. But their effect is to put an extra burden on those managers and senior staff who remain. Running public transport is a notoriously thankless task, exposing the operator to constant harassment and ill-informed abuse. If the public transport manager is to be efficient, loyal and – in the words of the old LPTB slogan – 'strong for service', then he must be given recognition and status at least as high as that of his counterparts in other areas of the public service. So it could well prove a false economy if the cuts in senior LT staff were to be paralleled by cuts in any of the personal privileges and facilities enjoyed by the managers remaining to run the undertaking. Without adequate management motivation, recognition and reward, no big undertaking – let alone a public transport organisation such as London Transport – can expect to keep a competent and enthusiastic team of managers in its service.

Let us now look at the effect of the ups and downs of the 1980s on the services operated by London Transport, and on the level of traffic carried on them. One factor which had bedevilled the services in the 1960s and 1970s – the shortage of operating and support staff – has virtually disappeared with the advent of large-scale unemployment caused by the economic depression of the past few years. Indeed, as we have seen, staff cuts have now become the order of the day. This, and improved rolling stock availability, resulted in a steady decrease in the percentage of the scheduled services lost (ie not operated) between 1979 and 1981, although there was a slight setback in 1982, largely attributable to a two-week strike by Underground train staff in June of that year.

Because of the doubts, after the Law Lords' ruling, about the level of subsidy that would be legal and the proper level of services that should be run in relation to level of demand, it was decided during 1982 to reduce the scheduled service frequencies generally on both the bus and Underground systems. These changes were introduced in the autumn of 1982, and actually had the effect of improving the regularity and reliability of services. On the buses, for example, it was shown that although services were scheduled less frequently after September 1982, their reliability was so improved that the average waiting time spent by passengers at bus stops was actually reduced.

As regards the level of traffic carried, this has gone up and down in response to the violent swings in fare levels in the past two or three years. The 32% Fares Fair cut in October 1981 resulted in a 10% increase in passengers. The 96% increase in fares in March 1982, following the Law Lords' ruling, resulted in an 18% decrease in passengers. The 25% Balanced Plan fares cut in May 1983 was followed by a 12%-15% increase in the number of passengers. In terms of calendar years, London Transport experienced a drop in traffic between 1980 and 1981, and again between 1981 and 1982, because in each of the last two full years the period of high fares has greatly exceeded the period of low fares. However, in the two quarterly periods during which the low Fares Fair policy operated – the last quarter of 1981 and the first quarter of 1982 – the passenger-mile figures clocked up understandably exceeded those for the corresponding quarters of the previous years.

When, in 1983, fares went back to virtually the same overall level that they had been in mid-1981, one could speculate whether, if Ken Livingstone had simply

Above:
Underground traffic 1965-1983. *R. Armstrong*

declared a fares freeze when he took office as GLC Leader, London Transport would not by then have been carrying more traffic than it actually was. In particular, a fares freeze would have avoided the 14 months of unduly high fares which followed the Law Lords' judgment; many passengers lost through excessive fares do not return to public transport when the fares are cut again to a more reasonable level.

Of course, the fluctuations in London Transport traffic levels in recent years are not entirely attributable to the big changes in fare levels. Other factors have included the simplification of the fares system, the changes in service levels and the effects of the economic recession on the commercial life of the capital. Some evidence of the last of these factors is given by the figure of daily passenger movement into Central London in the morning peak period by all means of transport, public and private, which went down from 1,069,000million in 1981 to 1,029,000million in 1983, ie by nearly 4%.

Traffic congestion has continued to cause major headaches for London Transport's bus operators during the 1980s, despite a more sympathetic attitude on

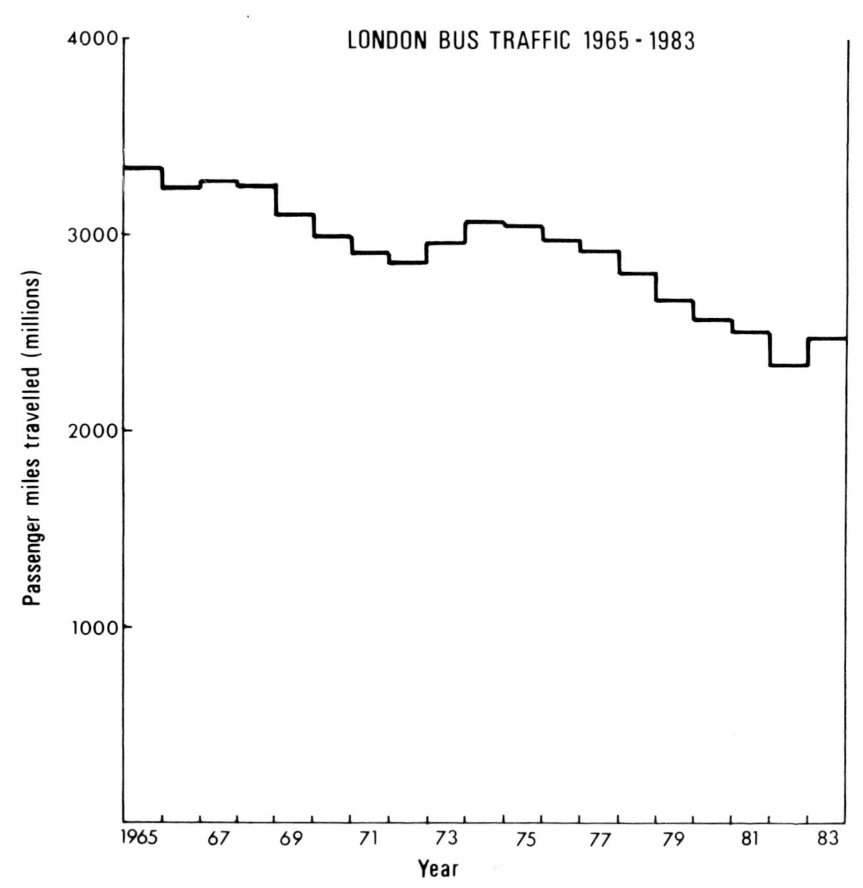

Above:
London bus traffic 1965-1983. *R. Armstrong*

the part of the Labour GLC, and indeed of the Department of Transport and the police as well. Nearly 3% of all scheduled bus mileage is being lost because of the cumulative effects of traffic jams, and much of the service actually worked is subject to severe delays for the same reason. In its continuing fight to win greater priority for the bus in London traffic, London Transport submitted a report under the title 'Make Way for Buses' to the new Labour GLC in June 1981, calling for a big increase in the number of bus-only lanes and special traffic engineering schemes. The early results of this new initiative were not impressive, the number of bus lanes in Greater London being increased by only seven (to a total of 156) during 1982; but many more such schemes were agreed or under consideration during the year. Moreover, a joint Council-LT experiment was carried out to give buses priority at traffic lights at seven junctions in Hounslow, using signals from bus-mounted 'transponder' devices to hold the lights at green or change them to green for the approaching bus. This year-long experiment showed that the scheme could reduce bus delays by up to 35%, and the results were considered so promising that a £½million plan was

Right:
London's version of the 'Denver boot'. GLC Member Paul Moore demonstrates the new wheel clamp in 1983. *LT News*

Below:
Too many taxis: a No 6 bus hemmed in by cabs in Regent Street. *London Transport*

announced in 1983, covering the introduction of the system at about 60 sets of traffic lights in southeast London and the fitting of transponders to a thousand buses, all as a first stage in a programme to install the system throughout the whole London area.

London Transport has naturally supported any proposals by the authorities at national or local level to reduce illegal car parking, which is one of the prime causes of traffic congestion in London. A recent measure of this kind, promoted by the Department of Transport, was that giving the police the power to use a form of wheel clamp – the so-called 'Denver boot' – to immobilise illegally parked cars. By the autumn of 1984 the Denver boot was reported to have reduced illegal parking in the areas of London where it was being used by some 30%.

But LT has pleaded for far more to be done to combat illegal parking and keep cars out of Central London and other congested areas, in the interests of the most efficient use of very valuable city road space. London Transport's proposals include higher charges for metered on-street parking, bringing the corps of traffic wardens up to full strength, and introducing a system of supplementary licensing or permits (road pricing) for the use of cars in the main areas of congestion.

Some idea of what traffic congestion means to London Transport in money terms was given in a report of the Bus & Coach Council entitled 'The Bus – the Key to Urban Mobility', published in mid-1983. The report said that it had been estimated that if London Transport's Monday-to-Friday bus services could operate under the same traffic conditions as its Saturday morning services, there would be a saving of £38million a year. In addition, the average speed of the buses would go up by 15%, and 50 million more passengers a year would be attracted to the more speedy and regular services, producing an extra annual passenger revenue of £12million.

An interesting initiative was taken by London Transport towards the end of 1980, when two new Airbus services were introduced between Central London and Heathrow Airport. At the in-town end, these two express bus services terminate at Victoria and Paddington respectively. Their success was sufficient to induce LT to launch a third Airbus route, between Heathrow and Euston, in April 1983. These routes were billed as being specially tailored for airline passengers with heavy baggage who might find the Underground service to Heathrow inconvenient. They were also heavily publicised in an effort to combat increased private competition to run bus and coach services between Heathrow and Central London, following the deregulation of express bus services in the Tories' Transport Act of 1980. However, to the extent that they may have taken some traffic away from the faster and more frequent Piccadilly Line service to Heathrow, the commercial case for the Airbus routes could be weaker than it appears at first sight; although the Underground remains far and away the most heavily-used form of public transport between Heathrow and the central area, it still has plenty of spare capacity through most of the day to take more airport traffic.

8 Fresh Challenges

The 1980 Act contained a number of other changes in addition to the deregulation of express bus and coach services; generally these changes were designed to make it easier for private operators to enter the bus business, or expand their operations, in competition with the statutory undertakings such as London Transport. For example, in exercising its duties as the licensing authority for ordinary stage carriage bus services in the Greater London area, LT was required by the Act to make a presumption in favour of new applicants unless it could be shown that their proposals were against the public interest. The Act also gave applicants to whom LT had refused an agreement the right of appeal to the Secretary of State for Transport.

Most of the new private road passenger services which have been authorised in and around London as a result of the 1980 Act consist of coach routes to carry commuters between the suburbs and their workplaces in Central London; these compete more with British Railways' suburban services than with LT's routes. Only four appeals under the 1980 Act had been allowed by the end of 1982, and in none of these four cases has the private service survived; indeed, in two of these cases, the service never even got off the ground.

The biggest challenge since the 1980 Act to London Transport's dominant position as the provider of bus services in Greater London came at the end of 1982, when a firm called Associated Minibus Operators Ltd (better known by its acronym, AMOS) applied for a licence to operate up to 500 minibuses on four high-frequency routes across London – from Wanstead and Leyton to Crystal Palace; from Muswell Hill to Sydenham; from Roehampton and Richmond to Ilford; and from Harlesden and Neasden to Plumstead. The company proposed to lease its vehicles out on an individual basis to AMOS 'associates' who would operate, garage and maintain them in accordance with overall service plans and standards. Passengers would pay a top fare of 70p for minibus journeys of over four miles in peak hours; for shorter journeys, and journeys outside the rush hours, lower fares of 30p and 50p would be charged.

LT's initial reaction to the AMOS application was voiced by Dr Bright. 'The minibus proposal,' he said, 'could have profound effects on existing bus, Underground and British Rail services, and on London's already choked road system. But it could offer a new type of public transport service to London. It is vital that all the pros and cons of this radical idea are brought into the open and fully debated.' As the licensing authority, London Transport therefore decided to set up a public inquiry under an independent inspector, Mr T. G. Holden, to consider and report on the AMOS company's application. Objectors to the AMOS proposals – apart from LT itself, in its operational capacity – included the Greater London Council, a number of London boroughs and the Licensed Taxi Drivers' Association. The Government, on the other hand, seemed to favour the proposals, at least in principle; in March 1983, the then junior Transport Minister, Reg Eyre, was quoted as saying that he would like to see the role of minibuses extended in a way that complemented conventional public transport.

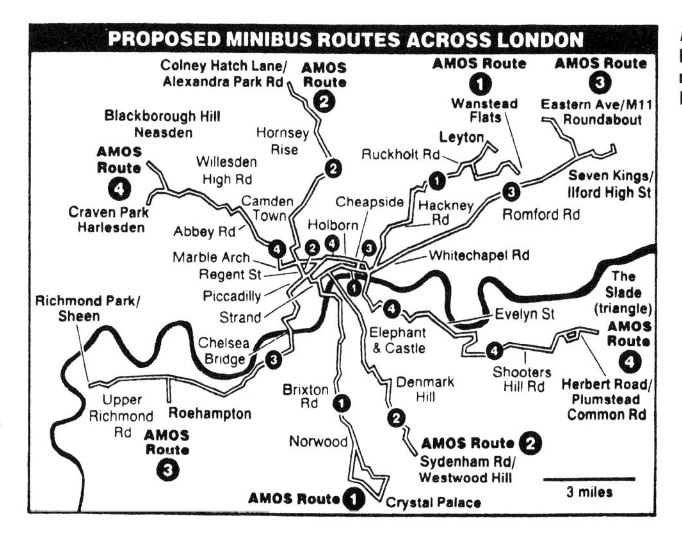

Left:
Proposed AMOS minibus routes across London.

London Transport's statement to the inquiry, which was held during the first half of March, contended that if the AMOS application were granted, there would be a setback to co-ordination and integration, inequalities in mobility would be increased, resources would be used inefficiently and the road network would be more heavily congested. 'Overall', the statement went on, 'the benefits to potential AMOS passengers appear to be outweighed by the disbenefits which arise across the whole of London's transport system.' LT also drew attention to some of the vagaries of the proposals. 'There is no clear evidence from the application,' said the LT statement, 'how the services as presently proposed could be operated to produce the quality of service promised.'

The case for the AMOS company's proposals was put to the inquiry by Anthony Shephard, the firm's technical director, who had previous experience of minibuses from his earlier days as a Commissioner for Transport in Hong Kong. He said that he expected much of the minibus traffic to be diverted from LT bus and rail services, although some would be won from taxis and minicabs, and at least 5% from private cars. He believed that LT was a 'sitting duck' and that it had no chance of improving itself from within.

Shephard was much less assured when he came to be cross-examined by London Transport's counsel and borough representatives on the operational details of the AMOS proposals. Asked about the performance of the minibuses, he said that they would average 285 miles a day at an average speed of 12mph. It was quickly pointed out to him that, if this were true, the buses would be running for just under 24 hours a day. Fortunately for Shephard, the inquiry was adjourned to enable AMOS to revise its figures. To secure a licence, AMOS had to specify the routes to be used, and Shephard was forced under cross-examination to admit that a number of the roads on the proposed minibus routes were unsuitable and that he had not consulted the borough engineers.

Some weeks after closing the inquiry, the independent inspector – a former deputy clerk of Oxfordshire County Council – submitted his 82-page report to London Transport. It was an unequivocal condemnation of the whole AMOS minibus scheme. The list of criticisms was formidable. Routes and terminals had not been precisely defined. There was no provision for turnround time at terminals, not even for staff breaks. The provision for controlling and supervising the services, as well as vehicle maintenance standards, was inadequate. There would be an adverse effect on congestion. The 'stop anywhere' facility was neither safe nor practicable, except possibly in the suburbs. The operation would be substantially less safe than existing bus services, because of the pressure on drivers to maximise earnings. Even on assumptions favourable to AMOS, drivers who leased the vehicles would at best make a very meagre income, and were in practice more likely to lose money. The AMOS financial forecasts were, in the words of the report, 'so optimistic that . . . they are best described as works of fiction'. Summing up, Mr Holden told LT: 'In my view, the disadvantages and dangers to the public are so overwhelmingly greater than any possible advantage that it would be folly to implement the proposals now before you.'

In the face of such devastating criticism, London Transport had no alternative but to refuse the AMOS application. In a statement on this refusal, Dr Keith Bright, the LT Chairman, commented:

'The decision was made not to protect a cosy monopoly for LT . . . but in the interests of London . . . We now have one of the most thorough reports on a licensing issue which we have seen. In the light of this indictment of the AMOS proposals, on many grounds including public safety, we have concluded that any decision other than rejection would be gravely irresponsible.'

Backing for the decision came from the London Transport Passengers Committee, the watchdog for passengers' interests, which had originally favoured the AMOS scheme. The committee's chairman finally conceded that 'it would have been the passenger in general who would have suffered' if the scheme had been allowed to go ahead.

Of course, under the 1980 Act, the AMOS company had the right to appeal to the Secretary of State for Transport against the London Transport ruling. It decided to exercise this right, with what results we shall see later.

Minibus promoters such as Anthony Shephard base their case on the success of extensive minibus systems in cities overseas, and argue that the same success should be achievable in British cities. But minibuses flourish mainly in Third World countries, where the standard of living is low, manpower is cheap, few families can afford a car, and the conventional buses are overcrowded and slow. This leaves a gap in the market which is admirably filled by the minibus. Such conditions do not apply in Western cities such as London, where there is in any case a vast fleet of taxis and minicabs to fill the gap between bus and rail on the one hand and the private car on the other. It has, indeed, been claimed that because no limit has been put on a number of taxis that can ply in London, the taxi fleet has now grown to such a size that it is beginning to exceed its proper role and itself contribute to central area traffic congestion.

As we have seen, the 1980 Act was designed to help the private bus operator to challenge the so-called monopoly of the big public transport undertakings, so the AMOS fiasco was scarcely a very good advertisement for the Act. Nevertheless, the same theme of increasing private participation and curbing the large operator is apparent in the Thatcher Government's second Transport Act of 1983. As mentioned earlier, this authorised the Transport Secretary to lay down guidelines on the size of public transport subsidies in Greater London and each of the other six English metropolitan counties, within which the subsidies could not legally be challenged.

The Act also empowered the metropolitan councils and the public transport undertakings themselves to order certain ancillary services, and indeed groups of actual transport services, to be put out to competitive tender. Moreover, the Act required operators to prepare three-year plans covering the level of services, fares and capital expenditure, together with a balance sheet setting out estimated costs, estimated receipts, passenger benefits and the expected level of subsidy. Operators were also required to heed the Transport Secretary's advice on subsidies and on the more efficient use of resources, and to supply him with any information that he needed to enable him to give such advice; in this respect, the Act created new direct links between the operators and the Secretary of State, by-passing the councils.

London Transport's first three-year plan under the 1983 Act, covering the period 1984-87, was submitted to the GLC and the Government early in June 1983. In his foreword Dr Bright said that LT faced a crucial choice – either to allow the pressures which had reduced the public transport demand (namely a shrinking population, increasing car ownership, and rising costs) to push the enterprise further into decline; or else to fight back to win more passengers, increase investment and provide again one of the best urban transport systems in the world. As might be expected, the plan put much emphasis on greater efficiency and productivity, which would be achieved by capital investment, cutting out unnecessary activities, improving methods of working and contracting out functions where this would save money. All these measures would save about £63million over the three-year period of the plan, and there would be a reduction in the workforce from 58,000 at the start of 1983 to about 52,000 by the end of 1987. As much as possible of this drop in staff numbers would be achieved by natural wastage and voluntary severance. London Transport suggested that capital investment, currently running at £150million per annum, should be stepped up to a total of £1,830million over the next 10 years, so that the system could be modernised and automated to bring it into line with other European cities' networks in terms of efficiency and attractiveness. In the plan, LT considered six different possible levels of annual revenue subsidy in the financial year 1986/87, ranging from the Transport Secretary's guideline figure of £105million to the GLC's maximum option of £338million. LT's own preferred option was for a revenue subsidy of £167million – just below that in the GLC's Balanced Plan – which would enable the level of fares to be kept stable in real terms (excluding inflation).

The three-year plan evoked an immediate and sharp reaction from the Labour GLC. Dave Wetzel, the chairman of the Council's Transport Committee, described the plan as 'disappointing', and told a meeting of the committee in June 1983 that he disagreed with many of LT's productivity proposals, particularly those involving cuts in bus and Underground train mileage, and the extension of one-man operation. These criticisms appeared to ignore the fact that the LT mileage proposals were rather better than those in the GLC's own approved Balance Plan.

The Conservative opposition spokesman on the committee, Cyril Taylor, said that in his opinion the three-year LT plan was 'excellent, faulted only by weak measures to reduce fraud'. At the same time, he pressed Wetzel to say whether the Labour administration at County Hall was considering the appointment of six new part-time LT Executive (board) members to fight the planned cuts and productivity measures.

Although Wetzel refused to be drawn on this point at the time, it was only a matter of a few weeks before the appointment of five of the expected six part-time LT board members was announced. The five nominees made up a mixed bag. They included Larry Smith, an officer of the Transport & General Workers' Union and a member of the General Council of the TUC; Arthur Latham, chairman of London Labour Party and ex-MP; a 35-year-old female lecturer on transport history; a 75-year-old lady writer on public administration and finance; and a self-employed businessman with interests in planning and transport. Under the Transport (London) Act of 1969, the Council was obliged to consult the LT Chairman before appointing new board members, who must in any case be 'persons who appear to the Council to have had wide experience of, and shown capacity in, transport, industrial, commercial or financial matters, administration, applied science, or the organisation of workers'. Whether all the new appointees measured up to this description is a matter of judgment; clearly the Labour GLC thought that they did, and it was the Council's view that prevailed in law. There was, quite properly, consultation with the LT Chairman on the appointments. Indeed, Keith Bright put forward his own candidates for the part-time posts; but these were all turned down by Livingstone and his colleagues in favour of their own nominees.

Not surprisingly, there were many who saw the nominations as a move to pack the LT board with County Hall stooges. But Ken Livingstone denied Tory opposition claims that the appointments were politically motivated. The purpose, he explained blandly, was to broaden the experience of the board and to give consumers greater representation on it. As for the sixth part-time seat – which would complete the LT board quota of 11 members set by the 1969 Act – Livingstone said that this was intended for an ethnic minority candidate, and that he had already received 20 nominations for it. This seat would, however, be filled only if all parties on the Council and the existing members of the LT board agreed on the candidate for the additional appointment. Commenting on this assurance, Dr Bright said: 'My initial reluctance to accept some of the GLC nominations, to the exclusion of those put forward by the LT board, has been mitigated by this positive step.'

As a footnote to the block appointment of the five part-time members, each for a five-year term at an annual fee of £3,500, it is worth noting that the nominations were made in the knowledge that the Thatcher Government meant to remove control of London's public transport from the GLC as soon as possible.

Mention has been made of the plea in LT's 1984-87 plan for an increased level of capital expenditure to help in making the system cheaper to run and easier to use. The great majority of the undertaking's capital expenditure in the 1980s has been devoted to replacements and renewals (particularly rolling stock replacements), rather than actual new works. Out of a total LT capital expenditure of £123million in 1980, for example, no less than £57million – nearly one half – was needed for train and bus replacement alone. Again, in 1981, rolling stock renewals accounted for £58million out of a total capital expenditure of £147million, and Underground track and signalling renewals were responsible for a further £18million of the total. During 1981, however, plans were being developed for two new rail routes. The first of these, the Docklands Light Railway, was conceived as a low-cost alternative to the eastern extension of the Jubilee Line, designed to spark off the regeneration of the semi-derelict area of the East End formerly dependent on the old London docks; it would consist of a 4½-mile east-west line from Tower Hill to Poplar and the Isle of Dogs, plus a 2½-mile north-south line from Mile End to Poplar. The second new railway being planned was an extension of the Heathrow branch of the Piccadilly Line to the new Terminal 4 of the airport; this would take the form of a 3½-mile single-track loop in tunnel, running westwards from Heathrow Central station and then turning southwards and eastwards to serve the new airport terminal and rejoin the existing Underground line at Hatton Cross.

In July 1982 the Transport Secretary announced Government support for the £25million Heathrow scheme. It was agreed between London Transport and the British Airports Authority that LT would construct the tunnels and supply the track

progress at Hatton Cross on the Underground loop to the new Airport terminal 4, 1983.
London Transport

Below:

The Docklands Light Railway project – alternative concepts from the Docklands Rail Study 1981.

and equipment for the new line, while BAA would build the station serving Terminal 4 at its own expense and charge LT a rental for its use. Parliamentary powers had already been obtained for the extension, and London Transport was able to shorten the planned completion period by no less than two years so that the line could be opened simultaneously with the new teminal itself in 1985.

In mid-October 1982 the Government announced its support for the Docklands Light Railway scheme as well, subject to a limit of £77million on the out-turn cost. Announcing the new line, David Howell, then Transport Secretary, said: 'This novel type of railway particularly suits Dockland's needs. It will be quicker to build than a conventional rail link, cost less to construct and will be cheaper to run. I have told the GLC that the scheme will be designated as one of national and regional importance.' Michael Heseltine, then Environment Secretary, was also involved in this decision because of his department's responsibility for the London Docklands Development Corporation (LDDC), which had been set up by the Government to revitalise the decaying riverside area. Speaking of the Docklands rail plan, Heseltine commented:

'This exciting project will provide major stimulus to the regeneration of London's Docklands by making the area a better place to live and work in. It will also make Docklands a much more attractive prospect for investment by employers and developers. I have agreed to make the necessary funds available to enable the LDDC to meet 50 per cent of the cost of the scheme.'

The other half of the cost was to be met by the Greater London Council. In November 1982, London Transport deposited a Bill in Parliament seeking the legal powers needed for the east-west Docklands line, which should now be completed by 1987. The second stage, covering the north-south line, proved more controversial, as the GLC favoured terminating it at Stratford station rather than at Mile End, even though this would add several million pounds to a financially tight scheme. The Docklands rail system will be of conventional light rapid transit type, with steel wheels on steel rails and manned trains, but with unmanned stations. A later third stage – an extension from Poplar to Beckton – is now being studied.

The Heathrow and Docklands rail schemes represent an actual expansion of the LT network, but there has also been increased emphasis on the physical improvement of the existing system in the past few years. In the autumn of 1981, for example, the GLC gave its approval in principle to a 10-year rolling programme to modernise 140 Underground stations at a cost of £60million. Of this sum, a substantial majority – about £40million – was earmarked for a mere 16 big schemes to make central area stations more attractive and more convenient to use; this concentration of effort on the large central stations, which together deal with such a high proportion of the total traffic on the Underground, echoed the theme of London Transport's previous station modernisation programme of the 1970s.

Other increases in capital expenditure in the last year or two have been designed to cut operating costs and losses due to fare-dodging. In mid-1983, for example, London Transport submitted to County Hall plans for what will be, in effect, its third attempt to get a workable and cost-effective system of automatic fare collection (AFC) on the Underground network. The cost of installing it over five years will amount to between £100million and £110million, but it is expected to produce a net financial return of nearly £15million a year. LT modified its initial proposals by limiting the number of stations to be equipped with tight AFC gates and barriers to about 60 stations in Central and Inner London. All the remaining stations, mostly suburban, will be run as 'open' stations, where passengers will themselves validate their tickets by passing them through a special machine. The cut in the costs of ticket issue, checking and collection, and the savings in fraud, will be partly offset by the cost of employing extra travelling ticket inspectors on the trains. In promoting the scheme, LT hoped that it would be given the right to collect on-the-spot fines from fare bilkers – a right previously denied it. The GLC Transport Committee was told that this so-called 'composite' plan offered the best value for money out of all the options available. Under the new title of 'Underground Ticketing System' (UTS), the first phase of the scheme was given the green light by the GLC Committee in June 1984.

In placing orders for 725 new double-deck buses for delivery in 1984 and 1985, London Transport has again aimed at saving on future working costs – in this case by a further extension of one-man bus operation where this will not be counter-productive. For the longer-term bus replacement programme, LT is trying out a different type of double-deck vehicle from each of four manufacturers. The purpose of the trials is to find out how much of a manufacturer's standard product can be used, without producing a special design of bus solely to meet London conditions; it is to be hoped that the lessons of the late 1960s, when LT was induced by Government pressures to buy buses off the shelf – with dire results – will not be forgotten.

The LT capital programme also covers the cost of developing and installing new equipment to enable more Underground lines to be converted to one-man train operation by the end of the decade.

Altogether then, there is a reasonable hope of an adequate injection of capital into London Transport in the coming years to make the system progressively more attractive to the travelling public, to increase productivity and to curb fare-dodging. Even so, the level of capital expenditure in London Transport will continue to fall far short of the French authorities' massive investments in the Paris public transport system, which have turned it into a showpiece and so helped France to win contracts worth billions of francs for rolling stock and other equipment for growing metro and bus systems in cities throughout the world.

9 A Chance to Get Things Right

So far as London Transport is concerned, the latest and most momentous development of the 1980s has been the Thatcher Government's move to take the political and financial responsibility for London's public transport system out of the hands of the Greater London Council. Much of the steam for this proposal came from a report of an all-party Commons Transport Committee on 'Transport in London' which appeared in July 1982. This Select Committee had taken evidence from a wide range of official and unofficial witnesses during the previous year, and had been helped in its deliberations by Anthony Bull, the very capable former Vice-Chairman of London Transport, who acted as independent assessor to the Committee; evidence on behalf of LT itself was given during 1981 by the undertaking's then Chairman, Sir Peter Masefield.

Briefly, the Commons Committee report proposed a new Metropolitan Transport Authority (MTA) to take over London Transport and the metropolitan road system from the GLC and trunk roads in the London region from the Department of Transport. The area covered by the MTA would be much larger than that of the Greater London Council; in fact, it would correspond exactly to the old London Passenger Transport Area, much of which LT had had to give up when it was put under GLC control in 1970.

It was proposed that the members of the MTA should be appointed rather than directly elected; but the new authority would be able to add its precept to the local rates bills. It was envisaged that one half of the members of the MTA would be appointed by the Transport Secretary and the other half by the GLC (if still in being), by the London Boroughs, and by the county and district councils in the ring between the GLC and MTA boundaries.

The proposed MTA would have the power to give financial support to both LT and British Railways, and the Committee suggested that the Government should consider the possibility of transferring responsibility for the payment of the public service obligation grant for BR's London commuter services to the new authority.

On the fares issue, the Commons Committee was disappointingly vague. 'The level of public transport fares', said their report, 'should be in the end a matter for political judgement for which the political authorities concerned should be answerable directly to the electorate'. In other words, presumably, fares in London would continue to be subject to violent fluctuations as one political party succeeded another in office. The Committee produced no ideas for keeping fares stable, such as an agreed percentage of subsidy, on the Masefield model.

On capital expenditure, the Committee proposed a massive increase in the budget for new roads in London as the outlay on the M25 ring motorway declined. For public transport, a much more limited increase in investment expenditure – 20% – was suggested; the money was to be devoted to new rolling stock, automatic fare collection and other infrastructure improvements 'specifically designed to improve the operational efficiency of the public transport system through reduced manning and increased ridership'.

Above:

Dr Quarmby of LT with David Howell, Transport Secretary, in 1982. *LT News*

On the very important question of public transport co-ordination, the Committee of MPs put forward the idea of a London Transport Operators' Partnership on the lines of the *Hamburger Verkehrs-Verbund* (Hamburg Transport Association, or HVV) and similar partnerships formed in other West German cities. The London partnership would have a legal status and would comprise London Transport, British Rail and the National Bus Co (which operates the London Country Bus Services system in the ring around the Greater London area). Its functions would include the physical improvement of interchanges and other links between the three systems, the standardisation of the fares structure and the co-ordination of services.

Reactions to the Commons Committee's report were largely predictable. The Transport Secretary, David Howell, welcomed the document, as did British Railways, the Bus & Coach Council (the trade association of the British bus industry), the British Road Federation, and the London Boroughs Association. Sir Peter Masefield, still Chairman of London Transport when the Committee's report came out, was concerned at the potential lack of business acumen and professional skill in the Metropolitan Transport Authority as recommended. 'At first sight,' he said, 'the proposed MTA would appear to throw together a large number of lay members who would have little transport knowledge or experience.' Understandably, the left-dominated Greater London Council saw in the Select Committee's report a portent of its own demise, and denounced it outright; the proposed MTA, said the GLC statement, would be a remote bureaucracy which would not be accountable to the ratepayers.

Whatever the shortcomings of the MPs' proposals regarding the status and powers of the suggested MTA, there is much to be said for their recommendations on the size of the new authority's geographical area. Extending London's transport boundary to take in the wide commuter belt beyond the GLC area would spread the burden of funding London's public transport and highway systems more fairly over those who use them. Under the present arrangement, a high percentage of the people who work in London live outside the Greater London boundary and commute to and from the capital by train, bus or car. So, although they put a heavy demand on the city's transport infrastructure, they make no contribution through their rates towards its upkeep. Giving the MTA jurisdiction throughout the original extensive London Passenger Transport Area should put that anomaly right, though the general taxpayer would presumably still be called on to provide some of the subsidy for London's transport, to reflect its role in maintaining London's value to the nation as a financial, commercial and tourist centre of world importance.

A wider geographical concept of London could also make good sense in other spheres than that of transport alone. In a television interview in 1982, Richard Brew, then leader of the Greater London Tory group, argued the case for some form of regional government to take over from the GLC and Home Counties the whole economic and demographic area of southeast England dominated by the influence of London. However, Mrs Thatcher and her colleagues subsequently announced their decision to abolish the Greater London Council altogether, along with the other English Metropolitan County Councils. This announcement naturally gave rise to an angry outburst from Ken Livingstone, whose own antics and intransigence were probably high among the reasons for the Government's decision. Less predictably, Alan Greengross – who had ousted Brew as leader of the GLC Conservatives early in 1983 – expressed his own and his colleagues' fears that the scrapping of the Greater London Council would leave a political vacuum in the capital. 'When restructuring comes', he said, 'we must ensure that London has a democratically elected body to provide direction for London's future, to give the framework within which things can be done and also to provide a democratically elected voice for London as whole.'

On 30 May 1983, only 10 days before the General Election, the Government announced its intention – if re-elected – of setting up a new regional transport authority for London, to take over control of London Transport from the GLC within about two years, ie a year before the Council itself was due to be abolished. The announcement, which was made by the Transport Secretary during a visit to Putney, was to be David Howell's ministerial swansong.

'It is time', he said, 'for a fresh, much more constructive and more imaginative approach to all of London's public transport system. We are determined that London Transport shall cease to be the political football it has become under the GLC. There must, of course, be full and proper accountability. This is very different from the ceaseless political interference to which London Transport has been subjected, leading to the chaotic doubling of fares and gross political mismanagement, especially under the GLC . . . There is the strongest possible case from the point of view of the London travellers and the commuter for a better deal and a better system than GLC control has been able to offer.'

There was little more in the Minister's statement to indicate the form and status of the projected new authority. It was not to be made responsible for the British Rail suburban services around London, but the Minister said that there would be close co-ordination between the bus and Underground services and the BR commuter network. It was clear that the Government was not going to adopt the 1982 Commons Committee's recommendation that the new metropolitan transport authority should take over all the capital's major highways. But there was no clue – apart from the use of the word 'regional' – as to whether another of the Commons Committee's proposals (namely to extend the London transport area beyond the GLC boundary, to embrace the whole commuter belt) was going to be adopted or not. The Transport Secretary did, however, specify that under the proposed new organisation concessionary fares would remain. He ended his statement by announcing that a Green Paper would be issued, setting out the Government's plans at greater length.

Within a fortnight of this statement, the General Election had taken place and, as expected, the Conservatives under Margaret Thatcher had been swept to power again with a much increased majority in the House of Commons. But the luckless David Howell did not re-emerge as Secretary of State for Transport. Instead he had to return to the back benches, and his place was taken by Tom King, who had been making his name as a quiet but effective Environment Secretary in succession to the charismatic Heseltine.

During his term of office as Transport Secretary, David Howell had gained an insight into the industry and come to understand some of its economic and social realities, unrelated to political dogma. If this contributed to his falling out of favour with Mrs Thatcher, it would not be the first time in postwar British history that a minister had lost his job for similar reasons. It seems to be a hazard of high political office in this country that as soon as a departmental minister gets to know the real problems of the industry for which he is responsible, and is starting to make a positive contribution to their solution, he becomes subject to the charge of political apostasy and is liable to be transferred or dropped altogether.

The importance that the Thatcher Government attached to taking London Transport out of GLC control as soon as possible was shown by the decision to introduce a Bill for that purpose in the first session of the new Parliament. At the

State Opening of Parliament towards the end of June 1983, the Queen's Speech included the bald statement of the Government's intention: 'Legislation will be introduced to reform the organisation of public transport in London.' It was announced that Mrs Lynda Chalker, who had survived the General Election as Parliamentary Under-Secretary at the Department of Transport, had been given the task of master-minding the setting-up of the new regional transport authority.

The Green Paper on the reorganisation, promised by David Howell before the election, turned out to be a White Paper when it appeared under different auspices after the election. The document was issued on 26 July 1983 and quoted liberally from the 1982 Commons Select Committee's report on the need for a 'determined national effort to relieve the crisis' facing London's transport system; for a 'face-lift to improve the reliability of services, the cleanliness and comfort of the services provided, and the ease of movement between one service and another'; and for recognition by Central Government that the improvement of transport facilities in London was 'a matter of national priority'.

But, as Howell's pre-election statement had foreshadowed, the Government's proposals did not by any means follow all the Select Committee's recommendations for action. True, policy control of London Transport would be taken out of the hands of the Greater London Council as soon as possible and a new transport authority – to be known as London Regional Transport or LRT – would be set up to assume responsibility for the management of the capital's bus and Underground services. But the new authority would simply take the form of a small holding company, with the bus and Underground systems as separate operating subsidiaries, and would be directly answerable to the Secretary of State for Transport, apparently without involving any London Borough or other council representatives. Moreover, the proposed new authority would deal only with public transport and would not take over any part of the highway system as the Select Committee had recommended; the White Paper said that the Government believed 'that the size, complexity and importance of London's public transport are such that the body responsible for it should have public transport as its sole remit'.

The White Paper also set out the arrangements for providing financial support for the new LRT authority. Instead of the past method, whereby London Transport has received grants partly from Central Government and partly from the GLC (in the latter case by means of precepts on the London Boroughs for the ratepayers' contribution), it was intended that all future grant for the new London public transport authority should come through the Secretary of State alone. Local authorities in London would be able to 'buy' extra services and to finance travel concessions for their own residents by agreement with the operators. With the promised demise of the GLC, it was suggested that the London Boroughs should get together to produce a joint scheme to be operated when they took back responsibility for concessionary travel for the elderly from County Hall.

On bus licensing, it was contemplated in the White Paper that the new LRT authority would be responsible for approving services and changes in services by its own subsidiaries and by other operators which had an agreement with the authority to supply services; road service licences would still not be needed for these services. On the other hand, a bus operator which wanted to run a local bus service in Greater London independently (not under agreement with the new LRT body) would in future be able to apply for a road service licence to the Traffic Commissioners.

The White Paper went on to say what the Government proposed doing to improve co-operation between British Rail commuter services in the London region and the bus and Underground services of the new LRT authority. In the first place, the Secretary of State would set up new liaision arrangements between the two bodies to cut out wasteful duplication, co-ordinate services and improve interchange facilities between their systems. At the same time, the Government would take reserve powers to enable it to transfer the support of British Rail's London suburban services to the new London public transport authority later, if desired; the need for this eventual change had been foreseen by the Commons Select Committee in 1982. The LRT authority would then become the channel for the public service obligation payments in respect of British Rail's London area commuter services and would thus be in the position of specifying the general level of those services, and monitoring them. With this extension of its powers, the new body would become a more truly comprehensive and effective public transport authority for the whole metropolitan region and its hinterland.

The White Paper acknowledged that the setting-up of the new authority's bus and Underground subsidiaries would be made easier by the form of London Transport's existing organisation, which was already divided into separately managed bus and Underground businesses. The new body would have to consider whether there was scope for further sub-dividing its activities in the interests of greater efficiency, particularly in the bus business; if it wished, and the Transport Secretary agreed, the LRT authority would be able to sell off any of these sub-divisions of its operations.

According to the White Paper, the new LRT would have four initial tasks – to 'improve bus and Underground services for London within the resources available and make the services more attractive to the public'; to 'reduce costs and the call on taxpayers' money and generally secure better value'; to 'involve the private sector in the provision of services and to make better use of publicly-owned assets'; and 'to promote better management through smaller and more efficient units, with clear goals and measurable objectives'.

Much of what the White Paper said was admirable; some was vague; and some again was rather naive, expressing pious hopes rather than a clear plan. Putting the new London Regional Transport Authority under the sole policy and financial control of the Secretary of State should avoid some – though not all – of the ups and downs of political treatment which LT has had to suffer over the past 14 years. It must also bring an improvement in co-ordination and collaboration between the new-look London Transport and the British Rail suburban system (even if the latter is not eventually put under the new authority's strategic control), since both networks would then be subject to the same political overlordship in the person of the Transport Secretary.

There was a recognition, too, of the vital role that public transport plays in the life – particularly the working life – of London. But there was no commitment by the Government to maintaining London fares at their current relative level. Replying to a question in the Commons on 27 July 1983, following the issue of the White Paper, the new Transport Secretary refused to give guarantees that fares would not rise in real terms after the new authority came into being; the answer, he said, would depend on the new body's performance. Of course, the Government is right in insisting on keeping public transport costs down; it might indeed be justified in demanding some form of regular and impartial probe into the adequacy of the new authority's productivity and cost-cutting initiatives. But there are limits to which costs can be cut without damaging the services to the public; and the panaceas offered by the White Paper – the involvement of the private sector and a move towards smaller operating units – are unlikely to contribute much in practice. Despite the official encouragement of private bus operators, many of them are likely to fall by the wayside, as others have in the past, when faced with the harsh economic realities of stage carriage bus operation in London. All told, they cannot be expected to make more than a marginal contribution to the sum of passenger movement by public transport in London. And for such of them as do hang on, there must be sound machinery to ensure that they do not 'cut corners' to keep in business by lowering maintenance and safety standards.

Also open to argument is the assumption made by the White Paper that, in terms of the size of operating units, 'small is efficient'. Certainly competition can provide a stimulus to efficiency. But it must also be remembered that much of the success of private enterprise has been due to the creation of larger, rather than smaller, organisational units – by expansion schemes, mergers and takeovers – in order to keep overhead costs down and benefit by economies of scale.

The White Paper also clouded the issue of the size of the new LRT authority's operational area. Talking of bus licensing, it seemed to suggest that the new body's activities would remain largely confined within the present Greater London boundaries. Talking of relations with BR, however, it implied that the new authority might one day have its responsibilities enlarged to cover the whole rail commuter network of southeast England. It seems a pity that, on this issue, the Government could not have taken the advice of the 1982 Commons Committee on Transport and fixed the former London Passenger Transport Area boundary as the most natural outer limit for all the new transport authority's activities and responsibilities; this would embrace all the regular daily passenger movement to, from and within Central London, with the exception of the relatively small proportion of long-distance commuters from such places as Clacton, Southend and Brighton. The main outer commuter districts within the LPT Area would then be making a greater contribution to the costs of London Transport than hitherto – as they should do – presumably by a rates precept on the Home Counties in respect of those parts of the LPT Area overlapping into their territories.

Going beyond this, one is tempted to envisage some sort of elected regional government to cover this much wider and more natural metropolitan area after the demise of the GLC, but with its functions limited to co-ordination and strategic planning. This would be almost guaranteed an on-going Conservative majority and would allay the fears of present GLC Tory councillors about an administrative vacuum after the abolition of the GLC.

Of course, adoption of the old LPT Area as the appropriate domain of the new public transport authority would mean that the London Country Bus Services undertaking could return to the LT fold – from which it should never have been driven in the first place – either as a third subsidiary of the LRT authority (along with the red buses and the Underground) or under contract to it.

A further unfortunate point in the White Paper was the adoption of the title of London Regional Transport, and more importantly its acronym (LRT), for the new public transport body. Throughout the world of transport professionals, LRT is already the accepted title for 'light rapid transit' (ie 'super-tram' or 'sub-Metro' systems of the projected Docklands Rail type), and the possibilities of misunderstanding and confusion are legion. However, past experience points a way out of the dilemma. The unified public transport body which has existed in London since 1933 has had a series of changes in its official name, status and size; until 1947 it was the London Passenger Transport Board; from 1948 until 1962 it was the London Transport Executive forming part of the BTC; from 1963 to 1969 it was the London Transport Board, answerable directly to the Central Government; and from 1970 to 1984 it has been the London Transport Executive again, but answerable to the GLC. Yet throughout almost the whole 50 years of its existence, the undertaking has been known to the general public simply as London Transport – sometimes abbreviated to LT – and has been identified by its universally known roundel sign.

So, even if the new formal title is 'London Regional Transport', confusion can still be avoided by following precedent and continuing to use London Transport (or LT) as the popular title and the classic roundel sign as the house logo. This has the added merit of avoiding substantial and unnecessary expenditure on redesign, repainting, reprinting and so on.

The main subsidiaries of the new authority are evidently to keep their previous generic titles of 'London Buses' and 'Underground', while using the general LT roundel sign. It would also avoid confusion if the buses of other operators working under regular agreements with the new authority carried the roundel sign as well, to show that they formed part of the general pattern of public transport services in London and that they conformed to the same operational, technical and safety standards as LT itself; and the operating and traffic statistics of these 'hired' buses should be included in the new authority's overall statistics, to reflect the fact that the services concerned were, in effect, being farmed out and that their operators were in the position of sub-contractors to the new LT.

In the debate which followed the Transport Secretary's statement on the White Paper, there was the usual exchange of half-truths and uninformed comment between Labour and Conservative members. Robert Hughes, the main Opposition spokesman on transport, saw the White Paper as a prelude to the privatisation of what profitable parts might be extracted from London Transport, and the encouragement of local private operators to cream off profitable services. His backbench colleague Norman Atkinson claimed that the Secretary of State had 'thrown all common sense out of the window and replaced it with political ideology'. From the Conservative side, John Hunt said that the proposals would be warmly welcomed in the borough of Bromley (which, it will be recalled, had successfully contested the Labour GLC's Fares Fair policy in the courts); Bromley ratepayers, said Hunt, had had to pay dearly for the politically-motivated cheap fares policy of the GLC. In similar vein John Page, Member for Harrow West, said that after the 'raping of the ratepayers of Harrow by the GLC over the past two years', they would be delighted by the Minister's proposals.

The reaction of the Labour administration at County Hall to the White Paper was predictably hostile in the extreme, but Ken Livingstone was able to find one small cause for a sardonic smile among the Government's proposals. If the Government went ahead with its plan to make the London boroughs pay the cost of free bus and Underground travel for pensioners, then – so Livingstone predicted – rates in 27 of the 32 boroughs would have to increase sharply; and the worst hit would be Bromley, the very borough which had first taken up the cudgels against the GLC cheap fares policy, with Harrow not far behind. Hitherto, the GLC has paid the bill for free travel for pensioners, after equalising out the cost between the rich and poor London boroughs. Without this equalisation process, the poor outer boroughs would have to increase their rates by up to 2.6 pence in the pound, while the rich inner city councils – including the City of London, Westminster and Kensington/Chelsea – would enjoy a rates cut of up to 3 pence in the pound.

One issue which Ken Livingstone stressed in his attack on the Government's White Paper was the lack of provision in the proposals for any direct say by Londoners in the running of their public transport network. After the General Election the GLC had commissioned Fieldwork International Ltd to carry out a survey on this issue, and a representative sample of 530 Londoners were duly polled between July 18 and 21, ie before the White Paper appeared. When asked if they

Above:
Transport Secretary Tom King takes Ken Livingstone's bus away – a cartoon from the *Standard* in July 1983. *Express Newspapers*

believed that they should have a direct say in fare levels and the quality of services, 84% replied yes and only 11% no. When asked whether they supported free public transport for the old and handicapped, 93% replied in favour. These results were grist to Livingstone's mill.

'The message is clear', he said. 'Londoners support reduced fares and want a say in their public transport system. The GLC will fight tooth and nail to halt the Government's plans, which will do nothing but harm to the bus and tube network . . . Fares will rocket and services will be slashed. At the moment, travellers can contact 92 GLC members about London Transport problems. How many will get through to the Secretary of State?'

There is an answer to this last question. Following precedent, the Transport Secretary will now have much the same degree of policy and financial control over the new London Transport as the Greater London Council has had over the previous LT undertaking. He will be answerable to the House of Commons for his control of the new authority's affairs, and there are 84 London MPs (and more if the new authority's area should be extended) whom London travellers will be able to contact about LT problems – and through whom the Secretary of State can be questioned on the discharge of his responsibilities for the new enterprise. Indeed, the creation of a separate forum of all London MPs to debate metropolitan issues such as transport has been considered by the Government. Moreover, taxpayers outside London and southeast England will in future have their proper say, through their MPs and the Transport Secretary, in the control of an undertaking which they partly help to finance. In addition there continues to be a watchdog body on the lines of the previous London Transport Passengers Committee to fight for passengers' interests and take up their grievances with the new authority and the Government.

In the light of these facts, Livingstone's protests – and indeed, the results of the poll ordered by the GLC – lose much of their force. In any case, it does not seem to have occurred to the GLC Leader that, to some extent at least, the Government's decision to remove London's transport system from the Council's control may be attributable to his own often immoderate actions and utterances.

After the publication of its White Paper in July 1983, the Government's next step was to invite the views of all interested parties – the operators, the London Boroughs and authorities bordering London, the public transport staff and the users of the services – so that they could be taken into account in drafting the detailed legislation.

When the White Paper was debated at length by the Greater London Council in October 1983, the Tories on the Council joined with the Labour majority in condemning the Government's plans for London Transport. The opposition transport spokesman, Cyril Taylor, said that the GLC Conservatives were implacably opposed to the transfer of responsibility for LT from the democratically elected representatives of London to a Government department. If, nevertheless, the transfer went ahead, they would resist the levy of a special transport rate on Londoners. Otherwise, residents in the Home Counties who used London Transport services would be getting a 'free ride' – a situation which would, he said, be grotesquely unfair. For Labour, the veteran councillor Norman Howard commented wryly: 'Lord Ashfield must be turning in his grave.'

Even the business community of London showed some misgivings about the plans set out in the White Paper. In its response to the invitation to comment, the London Chamber of Commerce picked on the co-ordination of London Transport and British Rail services in and around London as the key issue; on this subject, said the Chamber, the White Paper was lacking in clarity and detail. In its view, any reorganisation of public transport in the capital should have as its basic objective the establishment of a single comprehensive network covering BR and LT, and any new body such as the proposed London Regional Transport authority should include in its responsibilities 'the oversight of services provided by LT, BR, and the National Bus Company'. Subsidies should be directed to getting better co-ordination, improved interchange and through ticketing, so as to win business to public transport and reduce the pressure on overcrowded and inadequate roads.

The Government was not left in peace through the autumn to ponder all the protests and advice that it had received. New developments came thick and fast. For one thing, there was yet another change of Transport Secretary; in mid-October, in the cabinet reshuffle following the Parkinson scandal, Tom King was moved to the Department of Employment, and Nicholas Ridley became Secretary of State for Transport – the third man to hold that office within a period of only four months.

Another development concerned the AMOS company's proposals for a number of minibus services across Inner London, which, it will be recalled, had been turned down for compelling reasons following a public inquiry in the spring of 1983 before an inspector appointed by London Transport. The Government now gave a clear indication that it was not prepared to relax its doctinaire line on the introduction of private enterprise into London's transport network, however unpromising any particular private initiative might be. Despite the damning findings of the AMOS inquiry and the widespread opposition to the AMOS scheme (from private interests as well as public bodies), the Transport Secretary announced that he was allowing the AMOS appeal against the ruling to go ahead, and that it would be heard in October and November before a Department of Transport inspector. In due course, Vice-Admiral Sir Stephen Berthon was nominated for this role, and his first action when the appeal hearing opened in Central Hall, Westminster, on 26 October 1983 was to reject a call from the AMOS spokesman, Anthony Shephard, for an adjournment until the New Year to give AMOS more time to prepare its case.

Surprisingly, despite the fact that earlier AMOS calculations and estimates had been largely discredited at the previous hearing, Shephard announced that he would be relying on the selfsame figures in this second inquriy. Under cross-examination by LT counsel, Shephard admitted that the proposed minibus routes had not been agreed with the Metropolitan Police and that they had still not been discussed with the local authorities concerned. When LT came to give evidence, its criticism of the AMOS plans was severe. The undertaking's chief witness, Ian Phillips, said that the suggested AMOS services would flout the statutory requirement for integrated services, seriously add to congestion, and causc inconvenience and danger by stopping anywhere on demand. Moreover, by cutting into the revenue of competing LT services, they would lead to higher fares, increased subsidy, or the reduction or closure of public services not in competition with AMOS routes. Other witnesses for LT questioned whether AMOS would in practice be able to cope with all the day-to-day problems of bus operation, including traffic congestion, mechanical failures and last-minute sickness among drivers. One expert witness with a wide knowledge of minibus systems overseas who appeared for London Transport, David Silcox, said that in his opinion the proposed AMOS services would cut street capacity, worsen congestion, increase the accident rate and lead to the abuse of the licence conditions and the traffic and PSV driving regulations. As in the earlier inquiry, the objectors – representing both public and private interests – greatly outnumbered the AMOS supporters, and the weight of argument was clearly against the AMOS scheme. When the appeal hearing closed in November, it was difficult to see how any impartial assessor could do other than endorse the findings of the earlier inquiry.

Anticipating the results of the appeal, it may be mentioned here that Admiral Berthon's report condemned the AMOS company as lacking credibility and as being 'not a reliable organisation to whom should be entrusted the introduction of a new private operation which could set an important precedent for the future'. When this view was put to the Transport Secretary by his own inspector, he could hardly avoid turning the appeal down; but in doing so in mid-1984, he nevertheless registered his view that there was still 'a case for the introduction of a spirit of individual enterprise into public transport in London'. Apparently he had never heard of taxis!

Another development in the autumn of 1983 was the publication by London Transport of the results of a detailed review of the role played by the two big bus works at Aldenham (handling chassis and body overhauls) and Chiswick (handling the overhaul of mechanical and electrical units). The review concluded that neither plant was economically viable, and that savings of over £8million a year could be made if the work was contracted out. Moreover, the sites themselves could be worth £25million. The two works were uncompetitive, the report said, because of high overhead costs, reduced workloads and outdated working practices. Aldenham Works was particularly inefficient, having been opened in 1956 in a building of cathedral-like proportions (originally erected as a rolling stock depot for an Underground extension that never materialised), with a capability of dealing with body overhauls for a fleet of 12,000 buses of standard LT design; by 1983, the working fleet numbered only about 5,000 with a variety of designs. Interviewed on the report, LT's Managing Director (Buses), David Quarmby, said that Aldenham could not be made viable and was being recommended for closure; but he thought that perhaps 1,700 of the 3,000 jobs at Aldenham and Chiswick might be saved by re-establishing elsewhere such activities as could be made economic on the basis of smaller industrial units.

The Labour GLC was shaken by the findings of the LT review and prevailed on the LT board to defer the decision on closing Aldenham Works until its 8 November board meeting. The Council was in any case advised by its own officers that any LT proposals to alter its bus works strategy required Council approval under the Transport (London) Act of 1969. London Transport countered this by quoting a more recent statute – the Tories' Transport Act of 1983 – which made it a duty to 'explore external sourcing as an alternative to in-house activities'.

Protests at the proposed closures of the two bus works reached their peak on the day of the crucial session of the LT board, when a mass demonstration against the closures was held outside London Transport headquarters in Westminster. A police cordon kept the demonstrators from entering the building, but a few protesters were allowed in to present their views. After the demonstration, the crowd marched along Tothill Street to a meeting in Central Hall, Westminster, where Ken Livingstone was one of the speakers. 'In Nicholas Ridley,' he told his audience, 'we have one of those real Victorian dinosaurs. No-one should doubt that LT will be the subject of a number of sustained attacks by the Government to see what can be privatised.' But he assured the meeting that the GLC would not allow redundancies to occur among the 3,000 men at Aldenham and Chiswick.

While the protest meeting was going on, the LT board was deciding on its next step. Afterwards Dr Quarmby said that it had been decided that the present factory building at Aldenham should close.

'However,' he went on, 'we have undertaken that those Aldenham activities that can be made viable will continue on or near the Aldenham site. A joint programme of action has been agreed with the trade unions which will aim to make viable as many of our current works activities as possible. This will lead to a plan to be agreed for Aldenham's activities by 31st January and for Chiswick's activities by 30th March next year.'

The GLC subsequently welcomed the joint viability review by LT and the unions, but warned the board that the Council was thinking of issuing a formal direction to LT to ensure that no substantial change in the organisation of LT's bus engineering services and facilities should be made without the Council's prior consent. At the same time, the GLC cast doubts on the conclusions of LT's own reports on the viability of Aldenham and Chiswick, claiming that they were based on 'insufficient and inappropriate management data'; but when the subject was debated at the Council's Transport Committee meeting at the end of November, a letter from LT Chairman Keith Bright was tabled which rejected this claim.

Keeping up its pressure for cost savings, the LT management also notified the GLC during the autumn of 1983 of its proposed timetable for further extension of one-man bus operation, so that some two-thirds of the services would be single-manned by 1987 (with annual savings of £6million and about 1,000 job

Above:
Aldenham bus works: an end view. *London Transport*

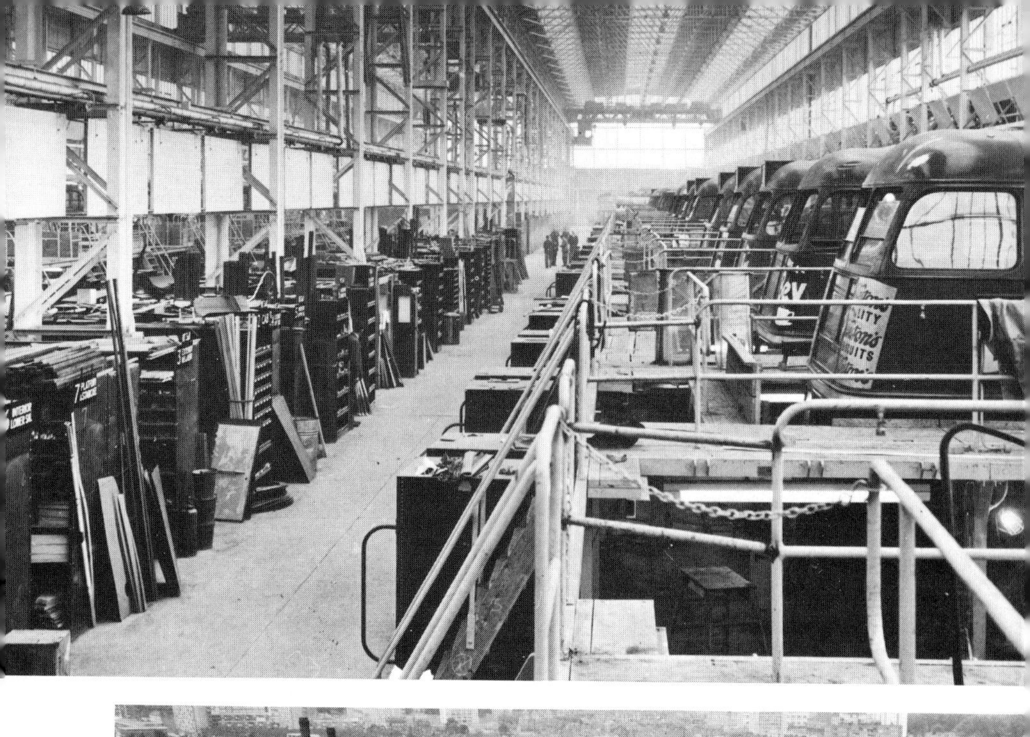

Above left:
Aldenham bus works: a view of the vast interior. *London Transport*

Left:
Chiswick bus works: an aerial view. *LT News*

Above:
Chiswick bus works: an engine shop. *London Transport*

losses), and the whole network would be single-manned in the 1990s. Earlier arguments had stressed the unacceptable delays at bus stops which one-man operation would cause on busy Central London routes; but these arguments were, it was claimed, weakened by the simplification of the fares system – particularly by the use of Travelcards – which greatly speeded up boarding on omo buses. However, the GLC remained sceptical and deferred a decision until it had had the results of a study on the subject which it had commissioned from a University don, Dr Phil Goodwin of the Oxford Transport Studies Unit. Dr Goodwin was asked to consider not merely the cost and revenue effects of further one-man bus operation on London Transport, but also its effects on bus buying programmes, the health of drivers, and community costs such as the bill for unemployed conductors.

The parallel question of one-man train operation – and eventually even unmanned trains – on the Underground also came up in the autumn of 1983. In his Presidential Address to the Railway Study Association in October, LT's Managing Director (Railways), Dr Tony Ridley – no relation, incidentally, to the new Transport Secretary – pleaded for the higher level of investment needed to extend one-man train operation and other measures of automation, and thus slash running costs. At the same time, he said, money must be available to improve the system for the passenger. An increasingly efficient but ever more tatty Underground was no more acceptable than a bright and attractive Underground whose costs were out of control.

While Tony Ridley was appealing for more investment to improve efficiency, his financial colleague Ian Phillips was pleading for greater stability on the public transport scene. At a conference in October, Phillips pointed out that since the Transport Acts of 1968 and 1969 British public transport had enjoyed the attention of nine Transport Ministers or Secretaries of State, six LT chairmen, four changes in the political colour of the GLC and a dozen Acts of Parliament on the financing or operation of public transport. 'That public transport policy has fluctuated so violently,' he went on, 'and that the usage of the network in urban areas has for the most part declined, suggests to me that we have not got our policy framework right.' In a later passage, Phillips said:

'All an operator really wants is stability in the financial framework and a degree of financial stability. We have had neither of these for at least a decade. A stock response to this problem is a plea for politicians to be taken out of our hair. But as long as we require support from public funds to meet the social obligations placed upon us, there will inevitably be political intervention, and rightly so. Our attention should turn to demonstrating to the outside world that supporting public transport is a worthwhile use of public funds.'

Dealing with the Government's plans for setting up a London Regional Transport authority, Phillips declared: 'The key aim must be to combine the merits of co-ordination with those of competition by the LRT specifying the level and quality of service it wants and then establishing competitive tendering for the supply.' Referring to transport services in other parts of Europe, he said that stability at comparatively high levels of support there had gone hand in hand with a more efficient and better used system of public transport.

Meanwhile the search for economies has gone on in London Transport, and the spotlight has been turned on the central management, professional and support services which have traditionally been provided 'in-house', to see how far they could be put on to a fee basis and could be supplied from outside LT where this would save money without a loss of quality. Excluded from this particular exercise are such direct support services as building maintenance and staff catering, although even in those areas some activities have been identified which could be run as separate business units or sloughed off altogether; for example, the Works & Building department may be established as a distinct business operating in the same way as a private contractor, and the catering department's Food Production Centre – familiarly known to London Transport staff for decades as the 'Croydon pie foundry' – has already been abandoned in favour of purchasing processed foods from outside suppliers. All these measures seem to be very much in the spirit of the Conservative Government's plans for the future of London Transport.

On the fraudulent travel front, too, London Transport has kept up the pressure, and in November 1983 it launched a £¼million radio, television and poster campaign to fight frauds by passengers involving losses totalling an estimated £30-40million a year. Early in 1984 LT was able to report that its anti-fraud measures had succeeded in cutting the annual fraud losses by an estimated £15million. On the Underground alone, the number of successful prosecutions for fraudulent travel had risen from under 4,000 in 1982 to over 5,000 in 1983.

In the meantime, thanks to better manning levels, more realistic scheduling to match available resources, more bus priorities and an improved supply of spare parts, London Transport was coming much closer to achieving its full timetable services than it had for many years. In the autumn of 1983, LT was able to report that in the year to date it had achieved over 97% of the scheduled service on the Underground and over 94% of the scheduled bus service. Traffic on the system had increased, too, thanks not only to the fares cut of May 1983 but also to the further steps that had been taken to simplify the fares system by extending zonal pricing and introducing Travelcards. A sample survey showed that the number of fare-paying passengers had gone up by no less than 12% since May, most (though by no means all) of the increase being experienced on the Underground. The survey also indicated a healthy reduction of 8% in the number of private car journeys, representing a worthwhile easing of traffic congestion and a real measure of benefit to the community as a whole. So good were the prospects that LT was forecasting a surplus of £25million or more for the full year 1983 after taking account of Government and GLC subsidies, and was even suggesting a fares freeze until 1985.

While many of the developments described above rated mention in the London and even national press, the piece of LT news which really hit the headlines in the autumn of 1983 concerned two controversial appointments to the LT board. The reader will recall that after a number of part-time appointments to the board in July, one part-time vacancy remained to be filled. The Labour GLC now nominated a 25-year-old black secretary and left-wing activist, Merle Amory, to fill this vacancy at a figure of £7,000 a year for a two-day week. At the same time they nominated 52-year-old Arthur Latham, a former Labour MP and a part-time LT board member since July, for full-time membership at £17,000 a year. This nomination was made following the departure from LT – with a 'golden handshake' – of an existing full-time professional member, John Cameron, who then moved to the Chartered Institute of Transport as its director-general.

Merle Amory's background was a highly political one. A secretary with the National Union of Journalists, she had become deputy leader of Brent Council within two years of election, and was active in trade union affairs, education, community relations and the West Indian Women's Association. She was known as a close ally of GLC Leader Ken Livingstone, and was reputed to have played an important part in the abortive attempt to get him selected as Brent's Labour candidate for the June general election in place of Reginald Freeson, MP. Oddly enough, Miss Amory was to lose the deputy leadership of the Brent Council soon after her nomination to the LT board, thanks to the defection to the Tories of another black West Indian woman councillor, and the resultant Tory take-over of the council.

Not unexpectedly, Miss Amory's nomination gave rise to angry accusations that the GLC was altering the balance of power in the LT board so that its political appointees would outnumber the professional members and change the board's policies. One full-time member was quoted as saying: 'If they vote together and block necessary measures to improve efficiency, our work will become impossible and there will be no point in carrying on.' Livingstone was also accused of breaking an undertaking that this particular vacancy would be filled by someone acceptable to the LT Chairman, Keith Bright. In a formal letter to the GLC's Director-General, Dr Bright questioned Miss Amory's qualifications under the terms of the Transport (London) Act of 1969. 'No matter how sympathetically one views Miss Amory's candidature for a board appointment,' he wrote, 'it remains true that she has only two years' experience as a councillor and no experience of management, corporate finance, industry, commerce or transport, and that her experience in the organisation of workers is already paralleled, and more extensively, by at least two other non-executive part-time members.'

Ken Livingstone's response to these attacks was to accuse Dr Bright of racial prejudice and to deny breaking any promises. On the alleged undertaking to appoint somebody acceptable to the board, he retorted: 'I only said I expected to. I was assuming they would take a reasonable attitude, but they are prejudiced.' Dave Wetzel, the GLC Transport Committee Chairman, backed his Leader's remarks. 'I would have thought they would welcome a black person,' he said. 'They have had so many dead-beats in the past.'

To the charge of racial prejudice in opposing Miss Amory's appointment, Dr Bright reacted vigorously. 'That is a ghastly accusation,' he said, 'to make against a body which on its own initiative called in the Commission for Racial Equality to make sure that there was no unintentional discrimination.'

Miss Amory's nomination to the LT board was raised in the House of Commons during the Prime Minister's question time on 3 November by the Conservative Member for Hornchurch, Robin Squire. In her reply, Mrs Thatcher said that she hoped that the GLC would take careful note of its statutory responsibilities to consult with the LT Chairman and to appoint people with the necessary qualifications and experience.

The Tory transport spokesman on the GLC, Cyril Taylor, suggested to the Transport Secretary that the Government should act at once against the GLC by rushing a single-clause Bill through Parliament to reconstitute the London Transport board, pending the setting up of the proposed new public transport authority. Although the Government did not respond immediately to this suggestion, the Amory and Latham appointments clearly spurred it to press on with its new draft legislation as quickly as possible.

Before Merle Amory and Arthur Latham could take up their new appointments on the board, confirmation had to be obtained at the full Council meeting in mid-November. The Council debate on the appointments lasted over four hours, during which time there were some bitter exchanges, including charges of racial and sexual prejudice. The Conservatives saw the appointments as a purely political move to block LT's efficiency drive. They were supported by Liberal/SDP Alliance members, whose spokesman, Adrian Slade, moved that the LT board should be reconstructed to increase its expertise in transport and business. But in the end the

Labour motion prevailed and the controversial appointments were confirmed by a majority of 44 to 41.

At the beginning of December 1983 the Government published its promised London Regional Transport Bill to 'make provision with respect to transport in and around Great London and for connected purposes.' The text of the Bill did not add greatly to what the Government had said about its intentions in the White Paper of July. The new London Regional Transport authority, referred to in the first schedule to the Bill as 'the Corporation', was to be responsible to the Transport Secretary on broad policy and financial matters, and was to set up two subsidiary companies to run the bus and Underground networks. Despite the title of the proposed new authority, no provision was made for expansion of the area of bus and Underground operations. Subsidies would be paid to the new corporation by the Secretary of State, who would recover up to two-thirds of them by means of a levy on Greater London ratepayers. Private companies could bid to run particular activities or services on an agency basis at reduced cost, and their bids must be considered by the new body and its subsidiaries; if their bids were successful, the firms concerned would get an appropriate cut of the subsidies. The new corporation would be able, in suitable cases and subject to the Transport Secretary's approval, to sell off parts of its subsidiary undertakings to private interests, including employees' share schemes, and the Secretary of State himself could order such disposals. The London Boroughs or other local authorities could have additional services in their areas if they wished, provided that they paid for them. It would also be up to the boroughs to decide on the continued funding of travel concessions for the elderly. The new corporation and British Railways would be required to co-operate closely, and the Transport Secretary would be empowered to transfer to the London Regional Transport authority later, if he so decided, the public service obligation for the BR suburban passenger services; if and when that happened, the new corporation would become the channel for the financial support to British Railways for those services. The Bill also provided for the two existing statutory committees representing the interests of passengers on LT and BR services in and around London to be replaced by a single London Regional Passengers' Committee.

In introducing this Bill at the end of 1983, the Transport Secretary, Nicholas Ridley, said that under successive GLC administrations – Tory as well as Labour – the cost of running transport had increased much faster than elsewhere. 'We have got to call a halt to this,' he said. 'It is quite clear that London Transport's services can be provided more cheaply and attractively.' It seemed, however, that the Government was not looking for early and massive savings from the new set-up; the aim would be to keep fares at their existing levels in real terms, ie to raise them by no more than the going rate of inflation.

Justifiably, Mr Ridley claimed that the level of political interference in London Transport had become intolerable; sensible cost-cutting plans had been rejected by the GLC for political reasons. But despite assurances that the new corporation would be left in entire control of day-to-day management, the Bill as drafted still offered plenty of opportunity for interference by the Transport Secretary.

The existing London Transport management reacted non-committally to the Government's plans. Doubtless with an eye to the future, LT Chairman Keith Bright said that it was up to the politicians to decide whether the Government or the GLC should control the undertaking.

Predictably, Ken Livingstone reacted angrily against the Bill. It was, he claimed, 'the worst combination of policies for Londoners' and would lead to a 'free-for-all', with fare rises and cuts in services. In particular he seized on the uncertainty about the future of free and concessionary fares for London pensioners, forecasting that the London Boroughs would not step in and continue the GLC's 'generosity' in this respect. The trade unions also weighed in against the Bill with dire forecasts of the numbers of stations that would be closed and bus routes that would be axed if the legislation went through.

The Bill had its Second Reading in the Commons on 13 December, when the Transport Secretary described the worsening fortunes of London Transport during its 14 years under the ever-tightening political control of the GLC. Referring to the Council's recent controversial appointments to the LT board, Nicholas Ridley said that he was expecting the next vacancy to be filled by Arthur Scargill, who at least had undoubted experience in underground matters. It was wrong, he went on, that the GLC should seek to turn LT into a political appendage of itself; and it was a scandal that the Council had mounted an expensive campaign to kill the Bill, dishonestly and recklessly using £850,000 of ratepayers' money for that purpose. Ridley stressed that LT was important in a national context, and for this reason the strategic control and some of the financial support should come from Central Government; in any case, ratepayers would be contributing less in the future than they were now. The need was for LT to be allowed freedom to manage its affairs with a minimum of political interference and control, but within clearly stated financial and policy objectives. The Transport Secretary also underlined the Bill's importance in providing the conditions for closer co-operation between London's bus and Underground services on the one hand and British Rail services in the London region on the other. The Bill would ensure that in future the two major operators in London would be subject to compatible policy and financial frameworks.

Ridley went on to attack a pamphlet put out by the GLC under the title 'Kill the Bill', which he described as reprehensible. The pamphlet told old age pensioners that if the Transport Bill became law, their free passes would be at risk. That was not true, said Ridley. Indeed, the London Boroughs Association had already agreed in principle to work out a scheme for continued travel concessions for the elderly in London, and to put forward proposals. His message to old age pensioners was: 'Don't be frightened by the GLC.'

The Transport Secretary closed his speech with a reference to subsidies and fare levels. He said that he had told the GLC that its protected expenditure level for revenue support to LT for 1984-85 would be the same as for 1983-84, ie £125million. This would not call for any substantial fare increases in the coming year, he said, provided nothing was done to add further to costs or block and squander the savings which the LT board was expecting to achieve.

The debate which followed Ridley's speech was not inspiring. Much of the Opposition's case against the Bill was based on the argument that it was wrong to take control of LT away from a democratically-elected GLC. One Labour MP, Tony Banks, representing Newham Northwest – also, incidentally, a GLC councillor – said that the Government wanted to take LT away from the GLC in order to make the case for abolition of the Council more persuasive. If the views of the GLC were not liked, it should be left to Londoners to decide through the ballot box. 'I would rather see a Conservative-controlled GLC,' he added, 'than no GLC.'

Not all Tory speakers were uncritical of the Bill. Tony Baldry, Conservative MP for Banbury, said that to allow anyone in London with a bright idea to run private bus services must inevitably lead to their going for the profitable routes. That in turn ensured that the losses on the loss-making routes were even greater.

The debate was wound up for the Government by Mrs Lynda Chalker, now promoted to the dignity of Minister of State for Transport, whose speech included an important passage on accountability. The Secretary of State would, she said, set out publicly the objectives and principles laid down for the London Regional Transport authority as required by the Bill, and his statement would be debated in the House, as would any subsidy.

At the end of the debate, the Second Reading was approved by 341 votes to 196, a Government majority of 145, and the Bill then went on to the next stages in the Parliamentary process.

1984 opened with a statement by Ken Livingstone underlining the commitment by his administration in County Hall to freezing London Transport fares for the next 15 months and increasing bus and Underground service levels above those proposed by LT in its budget submission. He said that the May 1983 cut in fares had been much more successful than expected, and that 15% more passengers were now using the LT system. The extra revenue coming in would enable fares to be held. This statement somewhat oversimplified the picture. Admittedly London Transport had ended the year 1983 with a revenue surplus of as much as £35million over the budget; but not all of that came from the effect of the fare cuts on travel levels. Some came from the simplification of the fares structure (especially the introduction of Travelcards) which accompanied the fare cuts; and some also came from productivity improvements and reduced fraud losses achieved by the LT board's initiatives.

1984 saw no let-up in the LT management's economy measures and plans. Early in January the number of district bus managements was reduced from eight to six as planned, and the headquarters organisation of the bus business at 55 Broadway was streamlined. Less than a week later LT released the results of a study of its main Underground rolling stock overhaul works at Acton, which showed that it had become uneconomic and would cost up to £42million to modernise. Little of the work carried out at Acton, said the study report, was competitive against prices charged by outside contractors. The study team concluded that much of the work at Acton, which has a workforce of about 1,000, could be done more cheaply at the rolling stock depots serving the individual Underground lines and should be transferred there. These findings were not unexpected, since the maintenance needs of Underground rolling stock have been greatly reduced in recent decades by the use of lightweight alloys, rubber suspension and electronic control systems, and the number of overhauls needed by an Underground car during its working life has been drastically cut.

The GLC reacted to Dr Bright's continuing economy and efficiency drive by making some further controversial changes in the membership of the LT board. At the end of February 1984, using the vacancy created when Arthur Latham had been promoted to full-time membership, it nominated John Palmer (information director of its Greater London Enterprise Board) as a part-time member of the board. At the same time, the GLC increased the pay of two of its earlier part-time nominees, Mrs Lewin and Ernest Rodker, from £3,500 a year for a one-day week to £7,000 a year for a two-day week.

John Palmer's background was one of active left-wing politics. Once described by *Socialist Organiser* as 'this well-known Marxist', he had twice had his selection as a Labour parliamentary candidate overruled by the party's national executive. After that he branded the leaders of the Wilson administration as 'traitors'. Then, in the 1970s, he figured in a bitter wrangle within the Trotskyist International Socialist movement. Before joining the GLC's Enterprise Board he had been European correspondent of the *Guardian* newspaper.

Above:
Acton rolling stock works: an aerial view.
London Transport

When Dr Keith Bright questioned these further board changes and the value of part-time board members, Ken Livingstone and his Labour colleagues gave him an ultimatum. If he was not prepared to drop his 'autocratic style' and work with the Council's political appointees on the board, he should resign. Matters came to a head after the board changes were approved by the full Council early in March. Bright, who had been on holiday in America, was summoned to a special meeting of the Council's Transport Committee for a showdown. Describing this meeting, which was held on 19 March 1984, the GLC Tory opposition spokesman on transport, Cyril Taylor, said: 'After Livingstone's ultimatum, there is no shadow of doubt in my mind that the Labour group were looking for the slightest excuse to ask Dr Bright to resign. It did not come because Dr Bright handled himself very well, keeping his cool, explaining things clearly, and promising to fulfil GLC policies. He did very well indeed. But Dr Bright's survival as Chairman depended on his continuing to abide by board votes, even though these could now be won by the majority of political appointees on the board.

The first test came at the end of the same month, when a new plan for the future of Aldenham works, agreed between the bus management and the unions and based on a new but smaller factory building on the Aldenham site, was put to the LT board. The discussion – which took place against the background of a recent Monopolies Commission report criticising the cost and performance of London Transport's bus workshops and garages – was long and outspoken. In the end the plan was endorsed by the board, but a vote had to be taken to add a clause ruling out any compulsory redundancies at Aldenham. Afterwards Dr Quarmby, LT's bus boss, who had voted against the extra clause, said: 'I am the last person to want to see compulsory redundancy, but I do not think it right to jeopardise the achievement of the difficult changes we face by ruling it out altogether'. Another clash between the two factions came in June. Against the efficiency-based plans of the professional members, the political nominees pushed through a GLC-inspired programme involving a fares freeze until 1988, increased services and a much-increased subsidy. Although the board's decisions were by then becoming somewhat academic, Dr Bright and his professional colleagues thought it wise to issue their own disclaimer after the meeting.

Meanwhile there were at last signs of a welcome break in the rail unions' resistance to more one-man-operated trains on the Underground. Early in 1984, after talks spanning more than a decade, the unions agreed to a three-month trial of one-man operation of conventional trains on the Hammersmith & City service of the Metropolitan Line. This trial was successful and by the end of the test period, running times were being well maintained. So later in the year one-man operation became a permanent feature of the H&C service and the Circle Line.

While these developments were going on, the Government's Bill to take over control of London Transport from the GLC was being pushed through Parliament as quickly as the legislative process would allow. On 28 March the LT unions called a one-day strike as a protest against the Bill and against the planned abolition of the GLC, but the call-out proved singularly ineffective, mainly because British Rail suburban services ran normally. Even 10% of the bus crews defied their union and clocked on, and the London Chamber of Commerce reported that over 90% of London's office and factory workers had got to work. From the GLC standpoint, the strike was probably counter-productive; among other things, it gave the Transport Secretary, Nicholas Ridley, the opportunity to condemn the Council for callously depriving Londoners of public transport for political purposes, and to refute Council claims that services would be cut and fares sharply increased after the Bill became law. During the report stage of the Bill in the Commons in early April 1984, Mrs Chalker dismissed as 'scurrilous rumours' reports from the GLC that the transfer of control would lead to the closure of 33 stations and 32 bus routes. 'There is no hit list,' she said, 'and there will not be. We have no plans to close down any stations or any route.'

The Government was so incensed by the GLC's campaign of misinformation against the Bill that it let it be known that it intended taking London Transport out of the Council's control as soon as the Queen had signed the Bill at the end of June, instead of waiting until October to create the new authority, as had been usual with similar Acts in the past.

When the report stage was resumed on 9 April, Transport Secretary Nicholas Ridley again claimed that the proposed new London Regional Transport authority would be able to increase efficiency and cut fraud, and accused the GLC of blocking savings to the tune of about £20 million a year which had been identified by the LT management. Labour's transport spokesman in the Commons, John Prescott, retorted that the Government's plans would make thousands of London Transport staff unemployed in the name of efficiency – implying that Labour believed that taxpayers and ratepayers should provide subsidies to help keep staff in jobs which had become unnecessary.

In the House of Lords, where the Bill had its second reading on 1 May, opposition spokesman Lord Underhill suggested, with some exaggeration, that the Government's plans would return the capital's transport to the unregulated mess of more than 50 years ago, before London Transport had been formed. More cogently, he argued that London was getting its public transport at a lower level of financial support than the capitals of most of the western world. He ended by welcoming a new provision which the Government had added to the Bill in the Commons to protect the future of the concessionary fare scheme for the elderly and disabled after the reorganisation. For the Government, Lord Trefgarne said – not without justification – that the arrangements made in the 1960s for the political and financial control of London Transport had not worked well, and that no one could be satisfied with performance since then.

During the Bill's passage through the Lords, the Government itself introduced an amendment making it clear that the new LRT authority's general duty extended to providing public transport facilities for the disabled; this is a potentially difficult and costly obligation. The Government also introduced extra clauses to enable the new authority to impose a minimum £5 penalty fare on passengers travelling without the right tickets who had had a reasonable opportunity to obtain one. Both changes to the Bill were endorsed by the Lords.

Interestingly, comparisons between London Transport and the Paris Metro and bus system were made more than once while the Bill was going through Parliament. The Conservatives pointed out that 58,000 staff were needed to run LT, while only 38,000 were employed to operate the Paris transport network, which was reported to handle much the same number of passenger-miles. This comparison was not a fair one, as a much higher proportion of the Paris system's traffic is carried on the underground lines and a much smaller proportion on the buses; and underground railways are capital-intensive while buses are labour-intensive. So the other side of the coin is that the Paris network has had several times more capital pumped into it than London Transport. Ironically, in the same year that the British Government was taking London Transport out of local GLC control, the French Government was planning to transfer control of the Paris system to the Ile de France regional council; on British experience, it could well live to regret it!

Left:
Mrs Chalker, Minister of State for Transport, beats the bus and tube strike on 28 March 1984. *Press Association*

Right:
Nicholas Ridley, Secretary of State for Transport since 1983. *Press Association*

With the passage of the London Regional Transport Bill into law, London Transport entered yet another stage in its chequered post-war history. Much will depend on how the new Act is implemented. Even before the Royal Assent was given, there were a few disturbing signs of the Transport Secretary's simplistic views. Early in 1984, for example, he overruled both London Transport and his own appeal inspector to open the door for a private bus service – Shuttlebus – to run between Heathrow Airport and any point in Greater London; and a month later, in a speech in Hampshire, he was apparently advocating free-for-all competition between public transport operators, in which – presumably – important but intrinsically uneconomic services could go to the wall. Then, in mid-July, he published a White Paper setting out the Government's plans to remove all road service licensing (so deregulating stage-carriage bus services completely) and to break up the provincial PTEs and the National Bus Co into smaller units – proposals which the Chartered Institute of Transport's magazine *Transport* attacked for their contempt for professional transport opinion and characterised as 'a stage too far too soon'.

The formation of the new London Regional Transport authority (only three days after the Act authorising its creation became law) enabled the Transport Secretary to give the GLC's 'political' appointees on the LT board their marching orders. Arthur Latham and his six part-time colleagues disappeared from the corridors of power in 55 Broadway. Dr Keith Bright and his professional team – David Quarmby, Tony Ridley and Ian Phillips – were appointed to the new authority with their status unchanged. And a full eight new part-time members were appointed, including David Hardy (an accountant, and boss of the Globe Investment Trust) as Deputy Chairman, together with Keith Brown (an investment analyst), Miss Eileen Coles (head of Unilever's commercial research subsidiary), Dr Stephen Glaister (reader in transport at the London School of Economics), Simon Jenkins (political editor of the *Economist* and part-time member of the British Rail Board), Mrs Helen Robinson (a director of Debenhams, who had chaired the British Airports Authority's design committee), Kenneth Joyner (managing director of Worldwide Estates and chairman of the LT Property Board) and Miss Patricia Steel (secretary of the Institution of Highways & Transportation and a council member of Age Concern).

This selection of nominees could hardly justify a charge that the Transport Secretary was packing the new board with Tory sympathisers. But there was no evidence of any relaxation of Conservative ideas on London's public transport in the letter which the Secretary of State sent to Dr Bright soon after the latter's reappointment, spelling out the Government's objectives for the new body. As might be expected, the letter laid great emphasis on further cost-cutting and improved efficiency.

'To reduce the present excessive call on ratepayers and taxpayers,' it ran, 'the burden of revenue support will have to be reduced. To achieve this, a proper priority for investment is vital. In addition to necessary renewal of assets, you will want to bring forward, as rapidly as possible, investments which will save costs and a steady programme to improve facilities for passengers.'

Reminding Dr Bright of his promise to achieve a reduction in unit costs of 2½% a year, in real terms, over the next few years, the Transport Secretary went on:

'I shall look to you if possible, to do better than that, and I shall want to review the target with you within the next 12 months. The most effective use of labour and keen purchasing in the market will be necessary in achieving this target . . . The improvement in efficiency can make a large contribution to achieve your prime financial target, which will be to reduce the level of revenue support from ratepayers and taxpayers to £95million in cash in 1987/88. Given control of costs, this does not in any way imply a programme of large fare rises. After any initial increase to redress the balance, I would expect you to maintain a broadly stable relationship between fares, prices generally and the fares of the BR London commuter services.'

On the development of the new organisation, Nicholas Ridley told the LT Chairman that he looked forward to receiving by the end of 1984 the board's proposals for establishing separate subsidiaries for the bus, Underground and other parts of the undertaking. After calling for the devolution of the bus subsidiary into smaller units and for a better match between supply and demand, the Transport Secretary told the new board that it must 'carry forward vigorously' a plan to bring in other operators, both public and private, to compete for the provision of services. This was an obvious reference to the fact that under the LRT Act, outside operators could not only – as previously – provide services in London under agreements with LT, but could apply to the Traffic Commissioners for a road service licence to operate independently of the new undertaking.

The first response to the Secretary of State's call for the privatisation of London bus routes came in October 1984, when the 'new' LT announced that it was inviting private operators to bid for 13 of its suburban and peripheral bus services, to see if they could run them better and more cheaply than LT had done. Bids for all 13 routes had to be submitted by early in 1985, and competing firms would have to show that they were capable of meeting satisfactory service, maintenance and safety standards. The bids would have to state the level of payment required to provide the services (including the operators' own profits); if a bid was accepted, the agreed sum would be paid by London Transport, which would in return take all the fares collected. LT's own bus subsidiary, and London Country, would be able to submit rival tenders themselves. It remains to be seen how well any private bidders do, both in matching LT's own bids and, if successful, in running an acceptable service.

The predicted figure of 7,000 job losses in London Transport as a result of the further productivity measures called for by the Government naturally incensed the trade unions, and they decided to put pressure on the new authority, and on British Railways as well, by calling for a one-day rail strike throughout the London area on 12 September 1984. However, thanks to talks between the unions and both managements, the strike was called off – though seemingly at the price of some watering-down of the two managements' productivity plans.

Strangely enough, at a time when there was heavy unemployment in the London area and further cuts in London Transport staff were on the cards, there was one job – bus driving – for which recruitment still posed something of a problem. This was not due to a dearth of applicants, but to the stiff qualifications needed for the job. So, although the recruitment managers were able to report that they were still meeting their targets for bus drivers, they were finding it much harder to do so.

Three months after the new LT authority had been set up, it released information on its proposed initial fare increases, intended – in the words of Nicholas Ridley – to 'redress the balance', that is, merely to catch up with inflation since the last change in fares in 1983. The rise being considered for the Underground would average 9% and would be brought in on 6 January 1985; bus fares would also go up, but the new scale for them was still being worked out. On the other hand, some fares beyond the GLC boundary would come down; these were those which had been increased under the GLC regime because the 'out-boundary' councils concerned would not provide the full level of subsidy needed.

Of course, inflation during 1984 meant that the real cost of travel on London Transport was falling during the year, and this gave some stimulus to traffic on the system. So also did a massive tourist boom, due in part to the strength of the American dollar against the pound; during the summer, the number of visitors to London from the USA was 20% up on the 1983 level, while visitors from Western Europe were 10% up. Ticket sales at Heathrow Central station – a useful barometer – were 12% higher. It was feared that an experimental ban on all smoking on Underground trains, introduced in mid-1984, might cut traffic and cause some enforcement problems; but these fears seem to have been groundless and the ban has markedly improved the Underground environment.

An interesting plea came from Conservative MP Matthew Parris in a contribution to the *Daily Telegraph* of 29 August 1984. He called for serious reconsideration of the 20-year old idea of road pricing – charging private motorists for using their cars in Central London – as the only policy which could make any real impact on the capital's grave and costly traffic problems. On the Government's plans for encouraging competition between buses in London, he pointed out that such competition was of limited interest and value if all the buses were in any case stuck in jams of private cars and taxis. Supporting the MP's plea in a later issue of the *Telegraph*, transport consultant Malcolm Buchanan (son of Colin Buchanan of *Traffic in Towns* fame) argued that there was no need to wait for the development of a high technology method of road pricing from abroad; an early but limited experiment with one of the simpler methods suggested previously should quickly show the merits of road pricing in cutting congestion and lead to its wider adoption.

Between the autumn of 1984 and the spring of 1985, developments affecting the 'new look' London Transport undertaking came thick and fast.

Dr David Quarmby and Ian Phillips, LT board members who had survived the political pressures of the preceding years, both announced their departure from LT – the former to Sainsburys, the latter to British Rail. This left Dr Tony Ridley as the only member with more than two years' experience on the LT board. The replacement for Dr Quarmby as the head of London Buses was John Telford Beasley, a pharmaceutical executive with no previous experience of the bus industry. At the same time, it was announced that David Bayliss, with long experience as chief transport planner of the GLC, was transferring to London Regional Transport as its director of planning.

In November 1984, the compensation being paid to the seven left-wingers appointed by Livingstone to the old LT board in the year before its demise, was announced. John Palmer alone declined the golden handshake. For the rest, the pay-offs ranged from £10,000 to £33,000 (the latter sum going to Arthur Latham). Merle Amory, whose appointment to LT had sparked off a major row, got over £13,000, and was almost at once appointed an 'equal opportunities adviser' with the GLC itself at £12,000 a year. The London *Standard* headline read simply 'Thank you, comrades'.

At the two bus works – Chiswick and Aldenham – and the main Underground works – Acton – the schemes for streamlining were pressed ahead. At Chiswick, three largely superfluous areas – the battery shop, woodmill and plating shop – were marked down for closure, and £8½million was allotted to restructuring the rest of the works to make them more efficient. At Aldenham, four new units began work in different sectors of the shops to cut costs and improve productivity in what was dubbed a 'battle for survival'. At Acton, more than £8million was approved for a new and smaller factory to overhaul train equipment; the rest of the work will be moved to the individual line depots. Using the same 'rescue' formula, a team was also put into the building department (now 'LT Builders') at Parsons Green to set it on the road to viability.

1985 opened with the announcement of London Regional Transport's first annual business plan, charting the way forward into 1985-86 and beyond. There would be over £240million in capital investment during the year, and the forecast revenue deficit of £128million would be £44million less than that of the previous year, and well on the way to the Government's £95million limit by 1987-88. Savings in manpower between 1985 and 1986 should amount to about 3,000, thanks to labour-saving investment and more single-manning of trains and buses. In the case of the buses, the management were aiming at 66% driver-only operation by the spring of 1986 and 75% by 1987. It was expected that all the staff cuts could be achieved without compulsory redundancies.

On 6 January 1985, the cost of travel on LT buses and the Underground went up by an average of 9% as planned. Dr Bright stressed that, overall, the new fares would only catch up with the inflation that had occurred since the previous fare increase nearly 20 months earlier. Of course, to achieve the 9% average, some fares went up more than others. At the same time, a new facility known as Capitalcard – a joint LT-BR version of the successful Travelcard – was introduced, opening up new prospects of coordination between London's two big public transport operators.

The removal of London Transport from GLC control in 1984 seems only to have intensified the feud between the GLC and the Government. Early in January 1985, the High Court ruled in favour of the GLC in an action which the Council had brought against the Transport Secretary, Nicholas Ridley, accusing him of exceeding his powers in asking for a subsidy of £281million for LT from London ratepayers in the financial year 1984-85. Mr Justice McNeill said that the Minister's demand was 'unlawful, irrational and procedurally improper'. The demand was, he ruled, some £50million too large. £10million had already been paid to LT by the Council; another £20million should have been met from LT's operating surplus; and over £20million for future leasing payments was outside the scope of the section of the 1984 Act covering GLC grants.

Nicholas Ridley's first reaction to the findings was to appeal, but at the end of January he told the House of Commons that he would 'shortly introduce new legislation to enable Parliament to determine once and for all the amount of grant to be paid by the GLC.' The Opposition reacted in fury, calling the proposed legislation 'a constitutional outrage.' And so the wrangling goes on.

Despite the continued problem of traffic congestion, London Transport entered its new state in 1984 on an upward traffic trend; but there must have been many qualms in the managerial ranks about the undertaking's future prospects under the new dispensation. Sadly, both major political parties have made serious mistakes in their treatment of public transport in London (and for that matter elsewhere in the country). Labour politicians rightly claim that public transport merits a high level of subsidy to prevent much greater losses through traffic congestion and disamenity; but they will not accept that taxpayers and ratepayers have the right to know that their money is being well spent and not wasted on overmanning and outmoded practices. The Tories, for their part, rightly consider that public transport should be run with maximum efficiency and minimum waste; but they wrongly think that this can be achieved by opening all areas of the business (not just supply and support activities) to competition – and despite lip service, they do not appear really to understand how vital public transport is to large sections of the community and how its encouragement can save long millions of pounds from being lost to the nation, day in day out, through the delays and frustrations of traffic congestion.

Although the London Regional Transport Act of 1984 has many shortcomings, it does offer the opportunity – if applied with wisdom and restraint – to get the organisation of London's public transport right for decades to come. It is to be hoped that the Government, despite some of its recent utterances, will make use of this opportunity by eschewing irrelevant political dogma, taking heed of informed comment, seeking consensus and genuinely aiming for a fair deal for the traveller, the taxpayer and the operator. Only by giving public transport a stable and assured future will London be able to keep moving and remain a lively, attractive and prosperous in which to live, work and play.

Index